CW01424536

# TOMMY BEING TOMMY

## Geoff Dunkley

First published in Great Britain

Pen Press is an imprint of
Author Essentials
4 The Courtyard
Falmer BN1 9PQ

ISBN 978-1-78003-801-8

Printed and bound in the UK

A catalogue record of this book is available from
the British Library

*It is quite something to be told by your*

*father of events and stories which took*

*place during the First World War, but when*

*corroborated by diaries which he himself had written*

*during the actual conflict,*

*a more authentic representation*

*of fact unfurled, and I am honoured by*

*my father's memory to share this*

*with you.*

# ACKNOWLEDGEMENTS

The author wishes to extend his grateful thanks to the
following for giving their permission to include copies
of photographs etc in this book.

## The Imperial War Museum - London

Ruins of the Cathedral and Cloth Hall – Ypres
(Ref No E(Aus) 1122 – Page 57)

Ruins of the Cloth Hall – Ypres
(Ref No Q.100470 – Page 57)

The Devastation of Delville Wood
(Ref Q.1211 – Page 110)

Troops passing the ruins of Fricourt
(Ref No 4084 – Page 112)

The devastation of Fricourt Wood following
saturation shelling
(Ref No Q854 – Page 112)

The Mire of Passchendaele
(Ref No CO.2552 – Page 171)

On the Road to Inchy
(Ref No Q7067 – Page 228)

## The Naval & Military Press Ltd

Unit 10 Ridgewood Ind. Park, Uckfield, East Sussex
(Excerpts from the History of the Lincolnshire
Regiment 1914-1918
Maps and Drawings)

# CONTENTS

# Official Terminology

## Translated into Tommy Jargon

| | |
|---|---|
| Senior Staff Officers Colonels & Above | Brass Hats or The Brass |
| Regimental Sergeant Major | RSM |
| Company Sergeant Major | CSM |
| British Front-line Infantrymen & Artillery Crews | Tommy - (nickname first given to British soldiers by the Germans as they believed that all British males were christened Thomas) |
| German Front-line Infantrymen & Artillery Crews | Fritz – (nickname first given in retaliation by Tommy |
| Trench Mortar Battery | TMB |
| Poor, Bloody Infantrymen | PBI |
| Estaminet | Drinking Establishment (Boozer) |
| Latrine | Brick Outhouse |
| Leave Ticket (Home/Britain) | a Blighty |
| Specially Constructed Junior Officers Front-line Command Post (in which they worked & slept) | Sap |

**The Dunkleys – a typical Victorian family**
**Market Harborough (Circa 1905)**

Standing (L to R) Fred, Ted, Arthur, Bert, Father
Seated (L to R) Harry, Emily, Mother, Edith, Frank

Five of the brothers served on the Western Front at the same time.

# PREFACE

This is the story of a young man's incredible journey across the battlefields of Western Europe during the darkest days of World War One. From attestation to demobilisation, the everyday world facts and figures have been collated from his own diaries, handwritten between early September 1914 and late February 1919.

Beginning the journey from a small picturesque village situated on the Lincolnshire-Leicestershire border, within a month of war being declared between Great Britain and Germany, it didn't come to its conclusion until four and a half years later.

The story unfurls through the early days of basic training, before setting forth to join-up with the British Expeditionary Force, which, at the time, was the largest to leave the shores of this sceptred isle.

Describing trench warfare, fought in the most appalling conditions imaginable, gives an intuitive perception of death and destruction on a massive scale. It also describes mud and bullets, as well as the continuous thunder-like noise of exploding shells.

It is also about unbelievable acts of bravery, above and beyond the call of duty. It tells of integrity and friendship, as well as self-conceit, arrogance, incompetence and power abuse.

Enlisting in the 7th Battalion Lincolnshire Regiment, for Ted Dunkley and his two best mates from the same village, it was all intended to be one big adventure, but it turned out to be anything but.

Although the story applies to one particular man's journey through Belgium and France, it could so easily relate to any front-line Tommy who served on both the Ypres Salient and The Somme.

# Ted Dunkley — author of the original diaries

# CHAPTER 1

## From Bothy to Barracks

The militaristic threat which hung so menacingly over Europe was at last activated, launching its mighty powers into armed conflict. Lands and rivers would be drenched in the blood of many nations as country after country became dragged into the maelstrom. No one knew when or where such horror would cease. Men would be hurled against men, inventions and science brought to a fine art to destroy the wonderful craftsmanship of centuries past, while millions of lives would be lost merely to satisfy the ambitions of a vainglorious few for territorial gain and the lust for conquest.

Every man, woman and child from cradle to grave had heard of the bogey – 'the Germans are coming' – yet still many predicted they would never come, arguing that war could not possibly happen in their lifetime.

Surely, they claimed, civilisation had advanced too far for mankind to attack each other should differences arise between nations. All that was necessary, they maintained, was a round-table conference between the antagonists, whereby any wrongs, imaginary or otherwise, would be easily rectified. Though, as everyone soon came to realise, such ill-considered supposition was nothing other than over-optimistic expectation, as those powerful Prussian Imperialists were hell-bent on world domination.

The spark which actually triggered off the first world conflict is well documented and so on the 4th August 1914, news flashed around the globe that a state of war existed between Great Britain and Germany. Arbitration had failed miserably as the Germans systematically broke all promises.

Already, Belgium was being overrun and in order to reach the Western European seaports, France was next on Kaiser Bill's invasion agenda.

..................................

In the picturesque village of Buckminster, it had been a glorious summer, so thought Ted Dunkley as he returned from his holiday, having spent it at his parents' home in the small town of Market Harborough.

Cycling back along the twenty-five-mile route, he passed through the tranquil villages and hamlets of Church Langton, Tilton, Twyford, Thorpe Satchville, Great Dalby, Little Dalby, Stapleford, Saxby, Garthorpe, Coston and then Buckminster. All the time, the windmills of his mind being unable to absorb anything other than what he himself could do to help his country in the great military confrontation, which he knew would very quickly escalate.

Ted was well satisfied with his way of life. He had attained the position of foreman in the Hall Gardens at Buckminster, after gradually working his way up from journeyman gardener at both Nidd Hall and Broughton Hall in Yorkshire. Being comfortably settled into his position and trusted, he hoped, by those above him, as well as those who worked under him. Well established until such time when he might have to seek pastures new in order to rise higher up the chain of command in his chosen profession, hoping eventually to become head gardener on a large private estate, then to settle down in life, a law-abiding citizen.

Having adapted well to village life, Ted was involved with sporting pastimes which all helped to make his life more agreeable. A successful summer of cricket had just been completed and now he was anticipating the arrival of the football season, to which he'd just been elected captain of the village club.

Upon reaching his residential quarters, namely 'The Bothy', he proceeded to his room before moving on to the common room, where other live-in gardeners relaxed after their day's work. Naturally, the main topic of conversation was war and all its implications. Everyone held their own opinions on the news in the daily papers, but just how long would it last, they all wished to know.

The world was thrilled to hear of the heroic Belgian soldiers and how they were managing to hold up the German hordes until help could reach them.

Britain did, of course, have a treaty with both Belgium and France, which guaranteed the sending of troops to assist in any emergency, if so required.

Making a powerful appeal for 300,000 volunteers, Lord Kitchener set the seed of revival in extreme national pride. What fit able-bodied young man could read those inspiring notices in the newspapers, as well as those placarded on the walls of every city, town and village throughout the whole country and not feel a great sense of patriotism? The army urgently needed resolute men and to their credit, men were responding all over Britain.

Every mealtime in the Bothy, the very same subject was up for discussion. Ted and his two best mates, Humphrey Rudkin and Tom Armstrong, exchanged opinions until the crucial question was finally asked, "What are we three going to do?"

The trio were naturally eligible for enlistment. Humphrey, an orphan, had no one dependent upon him, with the exception of elderly grandparents who lived at the nearby village of Sproxton. He had worked in his present position for six years and desired a change, so argued the three of them should join up without delay.

Tom, a groom at the Hall's stable block, was staying in the Bothy on a temporary basis and he too was of the opinion they shouldn't put off the inevitable much longer.

Ted, on the other hand, being slightly older than the others, erred on the side of caution, suggesting reasons for delaying any decision until more precise information was forthcoming.

During the next few days, the trio grew more restless over what they should do, until one morning at the breakfast table, they suddenly agreed their duty was crystal clear: they must answer their country's call. In any case, they reckoned it would all be over within six months, while some newspapers even predicted, it would not last beyond Christmas. And so, on Tuesday the 2nd of September, the three pals cycled the ten miles to Grantham to enlist in His Majesty's Army.

Riding along the Great North Road, they laughed and chatted like over-excited schoolboys, who had just knocked down a coconut apiece at the village-green fair, during Feast Week. At the same time, each one of them wondered what the future held in store.

Arriving at the barracks in Grantham, the three mates saw a large group of eager young men waiting to be interviewed, many of them from neighbouring villages against whom the Buckminster lads had fought encounters on football and cricket grounds. Now they were all answering their country's call to take part in a far sterner contest.

With medical examinations completed, Ted, Tom and Humphrey were passed fit for active service. Sworn-in with the necessary papers duly signed, they were told by a recruiting sergeant to report back at nine o'clock the following morning.

The final step had been taken and now there was no possibility of them having second thoughts, for tomorrow they would be soldiers of the King.

Returning to Buckminster, each one packed their few treasured possessions, leaving them with friends in the village until such time as they would be able to return.

Good God, if only they knew what was in store for them. Mercifully, the future was veiled.

Tom          Humphrey          Ted

..............................................

# CHAPTER 2

## Square Bashing – Etcetera Etcetera

An entirely new way of life began for the three village lads; soldiers for the duration, not one of them knowing for how long.

The parting from friends was not without regret, for suddenly they realised the step taken may well mean they were seeing their faces and shaking their hands for the very last time.

A party of over thirty lined up outside the barracks at Grantham, then under the command of an old soldier, they marched to the town's railway station bound for Lincoln, where they were to help form a new battalion in the Lincolnshire regiment.

Eventually Lincoln was reached, their documents scrutinised by military police, then still under the leadership of the old soldier, they formed up outside the station, to march to regimental headquarters. This was the trio's first appearance in the famous old 'Handicap' city, so as they strode out in purposeful fashion, mental notes were made of every public house, shop and café along the route.

Passing the racecourse, they noticed crowds of fellows in uniform, idling away their time, throwing out anything but cheerful remarks, especially about the atrocious food and poor state of accommodation at the barracks. These men had all recently enlisted, with seemingly nothing better to do with their time.

Reporting to the office for new entrants, the leader presented all the intakes attestation papers to a silver-haired officer, whose impatient glance towards them suggested an irritable attitude.

Sometime later, a corporal instructed the old soldier to take the thumb-twiddling party to a large building where they were informed dinner would be served. Following a further delay, the so-called meal was dished up and this really was an eye-opener.

Most certainly those remarks made by the groups of men near the racecourse were by no means exaggerated. It was little use complaining though, for it was a case of eat it or leave it, no one minded which.

It was certainly a discouraging beginning to the new life for the Buckminster lads, but although they were far from satisfied with conditions, all three had every intention of making the best of it.

Sleeping accommodation was woefully inadequate as no satisfactory arrangements had been made to cope with such a large influx of men in the space of such a short time. Volunteers were turning up on a daily basis from every recruiting centre in Lincolnshire, yet no one in authority seemed capable of knowing how to deal with such an unprecedented situation.

Tents were hastily erected on a patch of rough ground outside the Barracks and Ted, Tom and Humphrey, shared one with a group of new entrants who they knew from Colsterworth, Easton and Stoke Rochford. As no blankets were issued, they all slept on the grass, fully clothed in an attempt to keep reasonably warm.

The very same bungled maladministration was in evidence when daylight reappeared, long queues for breakfast with insufficient food to go around was an unsatisfactory start to the morning. Ted and Humphrey did, however, manage to acquire a basin of lukewarm tea apiece, with a slice of cold boiled bacon and a morsel of hard bread which needed a tenon saw to cut it, whereas Tom had to be satisfied with a single round of stale bread and jam without butter.

Everyone was mumbling and grumbling but when one high-nosed young recruit called out "I can't possibly eat this effluent," a company sergeant major retorted with "…welcome to the army, lad…. That's the best meal you'll get for a fair old while".

For almost a whole month, the entrants were given nothing whatsoever to occupy their minds and they made the most of it by wandering around the city in their scarlet tunics, striped navy blue trousers and black peak caps. No wonder those young Lincoln whippersnappers called them 'red herrings'.

Quite obviously, unsatisfactory arrangements could not last forever and eventually, after weeks of boredom, the lads were suddenly taken by surprise when barrack gates were closed and everyone was forbidden to leave. Every man was ordered on parade and given a somewhat serious lecture by the commanding officer. He made it abundantly clear that the undisciplined disorder which had been allowed to continue for far too long, had now come to an end, and that a strict programme of intensive training was to commence immediately. He then went on to inform the startled gathering that from that very moment onwards, it would be "Square bashing, etcetera, etcetera."

Within the hour, approximately one hundred men were marched to the racecourse, which they were told was to be their billet for the foreseeable future. Here they became the 5th Platoon, 'B' Company.

Yet again, Ted, Tom and Humphrey, managed to wangle quarters together this time in the saddle-room with several other recruits with whom they had made good friends.

There was Alf Wiggings, Arthur Atter, Jasper Houghton, Ernie Johnson, Alf Letts, Ted Paton, George Holmes, Tom Weller, John Hempsall, Charlie Cooper, Bill Dobson, George Rush, Bert Garn, Horace Hawley, Bill Gibson, Ernie Warner, Arthur Skins, Harry Haikes, Anthony Schofield, Joe Hollingsworth, Frank Gent, Charlie Watson, Harold Stokes, Arthur Brayshaw and Dick Keeble.

..........................................

To say it was much better at the racecourse than the barracks was expressing it mildly. Food arrangements were first class, as private caterers were called in to provide meals. Sleeping arrangements, though by no means perfect, were also a vast improvement. Subsequently, morale and attitude was high.

Training commenced in earnest. There was squad drill, section drill, platoon drill, extending orders, wheeling and skirmishing drill. With the amount of times the lads ran up and down that darned racetrack with full pack and rifle, it made fitter young men of fit young men.

Or, as most of the lads put it, "fit for S.F.A." or words to that effect.

# CHAPTER 3

## Bovington to Eecke

Having completed the first stage of basic training, orders came through for all recruits to assemble on the racecourse's rather mediocre parade ground, where the CO informed them that three new battalions would now be created – the 6th, 7th and 8th. All three were to be posted to separate 'trench warfare' preparation camps in the south of England, and 5th Platoon, 'B' Company – the 'Saddle-Room' contingent included – managed to stick together in the 7th Battalion under the command of Lieutenant Colonel Forrest.

In a way they were sorry to be leaving Lincoln, as several of the lads had struck up friendships with members of the opposite sex, of which the city seemed to have more than its fair share.

Rumours soon became rife that the 7th Battalion was destined to move to some remote spot in Dorset, and this was confirmed when, after a very long train journey which seemed to go on forever, they eventually pulled into Wool Station. Everyone alighted, formed fours and marched off to their new quarters which turned out to be Bovington Camp. It was a typical army 'cock-up', as no one at Bovington had been informed of the battalion's impending arrival. No food was readily available, so orderlies were despatched to local shops to purchase bread, butter, cheese and jam etc, with the lads having to contribute towards the cost, as it appeared camp funds were virtually non-existent. Eventually, tents were erected, blankets issued and yet again the 'Saddle-Room' gang contrived to secure their very own canvas accommodation.

Utensils capable of holding tea were conspicuous by their absence, so a group of the lads raided a nearby rubbish tip to rescue disposed-of jam jars.

Tent boards were an unknown luxury, which meant the ground was damp and cold, although each individual managed to remedy the problem by cutting bracken from surrounding countryside to make sleeping a shade more comfortable.

Quite a considerable amount of grumbling occurred, but the lads were well aware that life in the service would be no picnic. Or as those hearty sons of the fens would say, "no easy furrow to plough".

While the weather remained reasonable, everything was tolerable, but later on when the rains came, the entire camp became a quagmire. These, however, were conditions which the boys learned to tolerate, for they were elements which were only mild compared to what they would experience long before the war came to its conclusion.

Intensive training commenced, including long days of arms drill, section drill, battle drill, bayonet drill, rapid loading drill, route marches, physical training and lectures. Afterwards, the lads returned to their canvas billets completely exhausted, yet at the same time confident they were being turned into first-class infantrymen.

Christmas came and went and Kitchener's volunteers were becoming increasingly affected by boredom. The never-ending divisional training routines and route marches had long since lost any form of incentive. Some officers, realising the men were unhappy with the situation, agreed to remove certain restrictions and very soon the battalion was allowed to visit such places as Bournemouth, Poole, Dorchester, Lulworth, as well as local villages, hitherto out of bounds.

The time was fast approaching when Bovington Camp would be left behind and all those training rituals put into practice on foreign soil. The people of Dorset had treated them royally, so when the time came for the order to move out they did so with some regret.

The 17th Division, of which the 7th Lincolns were now an integral part, were bound for Flowerdown Camp at Winchester, where they were to be fully equipped before being dispatched to take their place on the battlefields of France or Belgium.

While at Winchester Ted, and several others, received orders to attend a machine-gunners course at Wareham. Lieutenant Burton was in charge and the actual assignment took less than a week, then it was a return to Flowerdown.

What a difference seven days away had made. Lieutenant Hayward, a young nineteen-year-old had taken command of 'B' Company and one of Ted's best mates, Alf Wiggins, had been promoted to sergeant. Humphrey Rudkin was now the Company bugler and Tom Armstrong was groom to one of the officers.

Every man was well aware that time was getting short and very soon orders would arrive for them to cross the Channel. All of them had been promised seven days' leave, but this pledge was rapidly rescinded, with all privates and NCOs being told it applied to officers only.

By now, the 7th Lincolns had merged with the Sherwoods, South Staffs and Border regiments. This formed the basis of the 17th Division, each unit being totally dissatisfied with the army's roughshod way of cancelling leave after being promised it. They resented such high-handed methods and weren't slow in letting their respective officers know of their discontent. They were not regular soldier class, as they had left behind loved ones and good jobs to answer their country's call, yet an ungrateful government was prepared to send them to the front line, probably to their deaths, without giving them the opportunity to say their last goodbyes.

Recognising he almost had a mutiny on his hands, the CO took the men's grievances to higher authority, the outcome being that each individual NCO and private was allowed a seventy-two-hour leave pass. Ted, Tom and Humphrey, together with the rest of the 'Saddle-Room' gang, made their way home via train and charabanc, but after having to change stations three times en route, both there and back, they only managed to spend one day with their families.

........................................

The great day finally arrived with the division being bound for France to play its part in making history, alongside those splendid regiments who'd been in the thick of the fighting since the beginning of hostilities but who, by now, were sorely depleted.

This memorable event had long been anticipated; indeed none of the men involved could understand why they had been kept back in England for so long. They left without pomp or ceremony, simply marching from Flowerdown to Winchester Station, where they boarded a special train to Folkestone.

The Lincolns were certainly a lively lot, bugles sounding all the way. One musical wit continually blew the 'Cook House Door' call, another 'Defaulter's Call' while Humphrey serenaded all and sundry with 'The Last Post'. A stranger would have been forgiven for thinking it to be a Sunday school outing to the seaside, instead of highly trained infantrymen on their way to war.

It was the 14th July 1915 when the lads of 'B' Company first set foot on French soil, all of them for the very first time. Through Boulogne's ill-lit streets they marched or stumbled, eventually reaching St Martins Camp, five kilometres outside the port. Rain fell incessantly, soaking just about everything with the exception of steel helmets.

A mere six hours' sleep was followed by an inadequate breakfast, after which each man was issued with iron rations before beginning their long trek to Belgium. The majority of roads on which they marched were cobbled, so naturally extremely hard on the feet. Although part of the journey was by train, two full days had passed by since leaving Boulogne.

Arriving at a place by the name of Eecke, they slept on straw in a large barn, real luxury for the first time since leaving Flowerdown.

Situated between Dunkirk and Armentières, Eecke was a small town with a couple of estaminets and Tommy being Tommy, these were his preferred ports of call.

The French customer's command of the English language was far from exemplary; even so, it was considerably more impressive than Tommy's French. Nevertheless, the two nationalities were soon able to make each other understood and a friendly rapport was quickly established.

Locals told the lads that an advance guard of German Uhlans had spent time in and around Eecke during their first mad-rush, proved positive by the graves of several of their soldiers.

Tales were told of how Fritz wrecked the estaminets just because the beer wasn't up to their own country's standard. Tommy replying that he could fully understand them doing so, as what was sold for beer was no more than good water spoilt. But at only the equivalent of a penny a glass, one could hardly grumble.

**'B' Company (No 5 Platoon) en-route march in the lovely Dorsetshire countryside.**

Ted pictured third from front (nearest camera) always maintained he was the only one in step!

# CHAPTER 4

## Baptism of Fire

Ten kilometres beyond Eecke, the Lincolns crossed the border into Belgium, each individual conscious of the fact they were moving closer to the front line.

Marching through Reningelst and Dikkebus, the threatening sound of shellfire became increasingly noticeable, as did the growing number of army ambulances passing in both directions.

On the outskirts of Ypres, the lads were brought to a halt and given a two-hour respite before Major Crawford gave them a final morale-boosting pep talk, stressing the importance of discipline. Indeed, there was to be no talking, no smoking and they were to move off in columns of four, but as the trenches were being approached, it was made abundantly clear it had to be in single file. Every man needed to be alert and it was imperative they keep up and not lose contact. The major also made it crystal clear that shelling may resume at any time, some men could well be wounded or may be even killed, but should such a mishap occur, the entire Company must keep going and not attempt to assist any comrade who'd fallen by the wayside, as stretcher-bearers would be close-by ready to help if needed. The major also insisted they all reach the trenches under cover of darkness, and that guides would be awaiting their arrival.

Ominous black clouds floated across the night sky, and as the order was finally given to move forward; the lads recognised the perilous side of warfare at long last.

All were unusually silent as they proceeded, each one having their very own private thoughts to keep anxious minds occupied.

It didn't take very long for Major Crawford's words of wisdom to be proved correct. "Always be prepared for the unexpected," he'd said.

Crossing over a bridge, which the lads later learned was the dreaded Bridge 14, the sky was suddenly illuminated by two brilliant flashes, followed by deafening explosions which seemed to burst amongst the leading men.

Dropping to the ground, not knowing what to do next, this was their very first experience of enemy shellfire. Fortunately, no panic ensued, although it was painfully obvious, some of the party would take no further involvement in the war, or any other war for that matter.

Stretcher-bearers were quickly on the scene and the rest of the Company proceeded as instructed. What a huge relief it was to learn that the shells had landed slightly short, otherwise the entire platoon would have been sent to kingdom come.

In single file, the lads passed through Sanctuary Wood, before dropping into a communication trench, where they were supposed to undergo further instruction. A constant fusillade of rifle bullets whistled overhead, causing distinctive thuds as they struck the charred remains of tree trunks. Suddenly, everything seemed like a hideous nightmare, but it was a frightening baptism of fire which would become increasingly worse as time passed.

Reaching the front line, 'B' Company was placed amongst battle-hardened regulars of the Scottish Highlanders, supposedly to learn the finer points of trench warfare.

Unfortunately, however, those men had been in the thick of it for four long weeks and were considerably overdue for relief. Highly delighted to see the new arrivals, their joy rapidly dampened when told they were newcomers from Blighty, who were only there for further instruction.

To say those 'old sweats' were a trifle disenchanted was the understatement of the century, as their selection of outrageous abusive adjectives and nouns, which they used to lambast all senior officers in the British army, was verifiable evidence of how the aphorism, 'swearing like a trooper' all began.

Ted, together with Alf Letts, Jasper Houghton, Ted Paton, Bill Dobson, Arthur Skins, Charlie Cooper, Harry Haikes and Frank Gent, was posted to No 9 Bay, but the look-listen-and-learn routine, as defined by infantry regulations, was by now a complete non-starter.

An almost exhausted Scottish corporal told the Lincolnshire lads to climb up into the firing platform and to keep a sharp lookout for enemy patrols, while at the same time, occasionally firing rifles in the direction of Jerry's trenches, "just to let the bastards know we're still awake, you understand", he added. Although just what he told the lads to do, should they happen to catch a glimpse of a high-ranking British officer roaming around in no man's land, was not for the ears of the pure in heart.

From the parapet, the new boys were able to take their very first goggle-eyed observation across the ungodly terrain ahead of them, with star shells and Very lights sent up by both sides at varying intervals to bring the entire awesome scenario into dreadful reality.

Being inexperienced in the subtle art of trench warfare, the small group were almost mesmerised by what they saw, and it was only after a sniper's bullet clipped Ted Paton's tin hat that they rapidly returned to objective existence.

It was a long treacherous night and although the lads from 'poaching' country had worked energetically during their stay at Bovington, no amount of training could mentally equip them for the actuality of the real thing. Naturally, the thorough preparatory work carried out back in Blighty was immeasurable, but with real live bullets continually whizzing past their ears, it was now a different kettle of fish altogether.

It was somewhere around 3am when Alf Wiggins, now Sergeant Alf of course, entered Bay 9 to pass on the order to 'stand to' immediately. This meant whatever anyone was doing, whether it was sentry duty, or trying to grab a few minutes sleep, at a given time pre-determined by the CO, each and every man in all trenches was required to be prepared to repel sudden attacks, as it was well known that most 'over the top' assaults were launched before daybreak, and on this particular morning Fritz was right on cue.

With rifles constantly firing, German infantrymen surged forward and backed up by mortars, obviously intended making a vigorous threat on British lines.

The number of Lincolns now operating in B9 section had risen to two dozen or so, and they all returned rapid fire. Not unlike sitting ducks, the enemy fell like ninepins, either killed or seriously wounded. The very same charge was made all along the line, but as quickly as it started, so it ended.

Delighted with their contribution to the half-hour commotion, the lads stood in the trench congratulating each other on their success. It was only when the short Scottish corporal put in his twopenny's worth that they came down to earth again.

"Don't get too carried away lads," he shouted. "If you think Fritz's officers are bloody stupid for sending out raiding parties knowing full well they'll get shot down like grouse on the moors, just wait 'til yer see what our brainless bastards can cook up."

The Highlander had barely finished the sentence when mortar bombs began to rain down close by, one striking the upper ridge of Bay 9, sending both Ted and Ernie Johnson hurtling rapidly into the side of the trench, before collapsing into the bottom. A heavy object landed across Ted's back and immediately he assumed it must be a wounded Alf Wiggins.

Pulled to his feet by Alf Letts, Ted quickly realised it was a full sandbag which had caused his anxiety, for there in front of him was the sergeant picking up the offending projectile with which to repair the rampart.

Suffering facial lacerations, Ted and Ernie soon realised they were only skin deep, and so both of them were able to continue doing their duty without the aid of medical assistance.

Just when it seemed the flurry of activity had calmed down, a huge barrage from British artillery opened up with ear-splitting ferocity, forcing Tommy into the trench bottom, in an attempt to muffle the horrendous disturbance. In response, Fritz sent over a solitary mortar bomb which again struck Bay 9, but on this occasion Ernie wasn't quite so fortunate.

Being seriously wounded, stretcher-bearers were on the scene in double-quick time and the last his mates saw of him, was lying on a stretcher being carried away. Although upset by the loss, the lads had precious little time to dwell upon the matter, as Fritz was still in an irritable mood and he needed to be made to see the error of his ways.

Mortars caused considerable damage along the line and many of England's finest sons would never again walk the country lanes and green fields of their homeland.

At 'stand-down' one sentry was left on duty in each Bay. Others kept their heads well down, some even managing to snatch a few minutes' slumber. Ted and Dick Keeble were initiated into the knack of making a fire without smoke, by using dry wood cut into thin strips, putting only a little on at a time, until the canteen boiled. How the lads valued those brief moments of inactivity, completely out of sight of what was taking place around them. Anyhow that tea was appreciated and so thoroughly deserved.

Throughout the day, skirmishes were taking place and both sets of adversaries caused each other troublesome predicaments, especially when their respective field-gunners decided things were too quiet.

Returning to sentry duty at 6pm, Ted found himself staring at enemy lines, no more than six hundred metres distant. Just as he was thinking what a lovely warm evening it was, a sniper's bullet grazed the side of his steel helmet, causing him to curse his momentary lapse of concentration. He was extremely annoyed with himself for not learning his lesson, after the very same occurrence happened to Ted Paton twenty-four hours earlier. It was, however, a lesson which served Ted well, for never again did he take the slightest incident in trench warfare for granted.

"Don't let it bother yer, lad," called one of the Highlanders, "if it's got your bloody name on it, well so be it, but if it hasn't, well you've got a fifty-fifty chance of surviving for at least another day."

Later during the evening, Lieutenant Hayward came down the trench to see for himself how the instruction period was progressing, only to find his lads had been in the thick of the action from the very first moment of their arrival. Far from happy about the situation, he nevertheless congratulated them on a job well done. Shortly afterwards, the Scottish Highlanders were sent back to billets for a well-merited rest period.

The next eight days were what old sweats always referred to as being 'nothing special to write home about,' which in reality meant death and destruction, as well as disillusionment, caused mainly by a total lack of sleep.

To begin with, the 7th Lincolnshire lads, or 'Poachers' as other regiments referred to them, thought it strange that a place with such an evil reputation should be so abnormally tranquil. The only hindrance being an enemy aeroplane which flew low over British trenches, its occupants, no doubt, observing the strengths and weaknesses of the defences. Eventually, the unwelcome intruder was shot down in flames by a superb display of airmanship by a British pilot. How the lads cheered! It was almost as if their favourite team had just scored the winning goal in an FA cup final.

A somewhat quiet night was suddenly rudely interrupted at about 3am when huge luminous flames leaped sky-high above trenches close to Sanctuary Wood, which were occupied by Sherwood Foresters.

Within a split second, this was followed by the deafening noise from minenwerfer explosions and German artillery fire in full blast.

It was an evil dawn with the repulsive odour of death, destruction, fire and gun smoke merging to suggest the handiwork of the devil was involved. Speculation as to exactly what happened went on for some considerable time, but it was quite a while later before it was confirmed that Fritz had used 'liquid fire' for the very first time.

A great many admirable young men were completely wiped out and troopers of the 8th Battalion, King's Royal Rifles, who were brought in to reinforce the obliterated Sherwoods, were themselves almost entirely annihilated.

For two whole days and nights Jerry was in an offensive mood, making it virtually impossible for stretcher-bearers to bring in the wounded. Occasionally, the faint cries of help from dying men could be heard coming from no man's land, and this, more so than shells and bullets, upset the lads.

When darkness again fell, Sergeant Alf Wiggins asked Ted if he'd go 'over the top' with him to try and recover a wounded man who must have been blown out of his own trench the previous morning. It was assumed he'd feigned death during the daytime, but seemingly totally disorientated, had managed to drag himself nearer to the Lincolns' trench than his own.

Slithering adder-like through desolate defoliated terrain, they almost reached him, just as a Very light burst above them, for a couple of minutes, which seemed like an eternity, the pair of them lay motionless. Just as they were able to move again, a huge rat scampered away from the prostrate body, from which it was enjoying a meal of congealed blood that had oozed from a deep wound several hours earlier.

With considerable difficulty the two rescuers managed to lift the unconscious man and carry him back to the trench, where he was treated by newly arrived stretcher-bearers, before being taken away.

While Alf and Ted were on their rescue mission, courageous comrades had managed to negotiate a barrage of shells in the rear to bring in the rations, and much to the delight of all at Bay 9, there were also letters and parcels from home. The way they scoffed bully beef with strawberry jam had to be seen to be believed. Then for 'afters', they all sat in the trench bottom and demolished a very large fruit cake, made by a devoted mother back in Bourne.

For two whole weeks, Fritz seemed to have held the upper hand, but gradually the tide of effectiveness was beginning to turn. An enormous British gun was brought into the action and this maintained a constant bombardment on enemy positions, each shell bursting with incredible accuracy.

After sixteen days of ducking and diving from strategic shelling, sniping and almost incessant rifle fire, allied to noise, death and destruction, the 'Poachers' received orders to 'stand down'. Tired and bedraggled, they trudged through shell-holed fields to billets at Poperinge. What was intended to be forty-eight hours of instruction turned out to be over two weeks of living hell.

Taking off their boots for the first time in their 'baptism of fire' period, and being able to sit in the extra-large concrete bath, was a marvellous experience, but suddenly all they wanted to do was to sleep unhindered for a whole month.

# CHAPTER 5

## Rude Awakening

Despite not being officially recognised as a hard-and-fast rule, all men, when relieved from front-line duty, were usually allowed a seventy-two-hour reprieve from any form of assignment, but of course, this was the British Army and their way of doing things rarely meant that Tommy was given much consideration. Young, well-intentioned officers may have directed trench-war operations with a certain textbook capability, but the old military authoritarians, who'd never before been involved in anything other than the vain pomposity of parade-ground ritual, were still a force to be reckoned with when it came to tradition.

Completely exhausted, B Company dropped into their spartan quarters shortly after midnight, yet less than seven hours later, they were awakened by the vulgar, loud-mouthed rantings of an old-fashioned, parade-ground CSM who barked out insults like some demented barbarian. All the lads were still fast asleep when the intruder entered, but within a matter of seconds the entire billet was in wild confusion.

"Right then you 'orrible cretins," he yelled, "didn't any of you hear reveille this morning? And what's more, you missed roll-call, followed by kit inspection. Where the bloody flamin' 'ell were you?"

Built like the proverbial brick outhouse, with a face like a Neanderthal man, sporting an extra-long upturned, waxed moustache that wouldn't have looked out of place on the head of a Highland bullock, the over-officious

NCO acted like a typical nineteenth-century, parade-ground bully. Intellectually sub-normal, he had obviously reached the pinnacle of his long but undistinguished career by ingratiating himself to like-minded officer class, who'd served Queen and country in India and South Africa.

Popeyed with disbelief at what they were being subjected to, the lads protested vehemently, although regrettably such defiance fell on deaf ears.

"Right then, I want all of you – and I do mean *all* of you – out on that bloody parade ground within fifteen bloody minutes. Anybody missing will be on a bloody fizzer and up before the CO, are you getting that?"

"Am I on parade, Sergeant Major?" queried Alf Letts.

"Why, what's so bloody special about you, then?"

"Er, I'm an orderly man, Sergeant Major."

"Of course you're bloody well on it, crafty bugger."

"How about me, Sergeant Major?" asked Arthur Atter.

"Why? Are you summat bloody special?"

"Officer's servant, Sergeant Major."

"Officer's bloody servant… of course you're on it!" snapped the Neanderthal. "Lot of bloody scroungers, all of 'em."

By now the NCO's face was white with rage, but when Bert Garn recited the unofficial ruling about men being excused duties for at least seventy-two hours, especially after having spent the previous 16 days in the front line, it turned beetroot red.

"And who the bloody 'ell are you then? Some bloody crackpot, no doubt," he raged. Then, in a slightly less outrageous manner, he continued, "Since when have bloody trainees under forty-eight hours connection-trench instruction been classed as front-line infantrymen?"

Muttering away to each other about the unfairness of the situation caused Neanderthal to continue his mentally deranged outbursts.

"I don't know what you bloody riff-raff are complaining about," he yelled. "This bloody shindig's a tea party compared to the fighting I went through. Mind you, it were real soldiering in them days though. There were nobody there to wet nurse us, you know."

Some wag, trying his utmost to antagonise the tyrannical NCO even further, asked, "Where did you do your front-line fighting then, Sergeant Major?"

"Me, lad? I was fighting in Baghdad when you bloody lot were still in your dad's bag."

"I didn't realise the Lincolns had ever served in Iraq, Sergeant Major," retorted the humorist.

"Well, if this Iraq's anywhere near the Sudan, then I can assure you, they bloody well did."

"Err, well, actually Sergeant Major, Baghdad's the capital of Iraq, and Iraq is nowhere near the Sudan."

This comment really rattled Neanderthal, and he retorted, "Oh I see, we've gorra bloody know-all amongst us 'ave we? No doubt you were a bloody comedian as well as a bloody smart-arse afore you enlisted."

"Well, not exactly Sergeant Major, I was a geography teacher."

With dishevelled, unwashed uniforms and boots which resembled those of a Folkingham farmer, after he'd been following shire horses and plough on a wet day, 'B' Company formed up on the temporary parade ground outside the billets at eight o'clock. Neanderthal was awaiting their arrival and he began screeching offensive remarks about their appalling appearance, just as Major Crawford, the commanding officer and Lieutenant Hayward arrived on the scene.

"Why are the men on parade, Sergeant Major?" shouted the Major, his monocle twitching like a kettle lid when on the boil.

Neanderthal's reply was cut short halfway through and the rollicking he received was poetic justice to the ears of everyone on parade.

Major Crawford apologised to the gathering and told them they were excused all duties for a further three days. Later, it was revealed that Ted Paton had managed to contact Sergeant Wiggins, who in turn alerted Lieutenant Hayward, and in next to no time, he was able to inform the CO of the miscarriage of justice which was taking place.

..........................................

Following the three days' rest, kit cleaning, physical training and route marches were the order of the day – anything, in fact, which kept the lads inactive minds occupied. On the other hand, by visiting the local estaminets, they did everything they could to keep occupied minds inactive.

An end of the week, route march took the entire battalion through Sint-Jan-Ter-Biezen and Klooster, before returning through the centre of Poperinge, where young children marched alongside, some even venturing to hold the lads hands. How much they all appreciated such precious moments away from the horrors of the battlefield. Occasionally, military vehicles passed by on the way to Ypres, but whereas the sound of distant gunfire was a grim reminder of the reason for their being there, it was still hard to imagine that hell with the lid off was only a few kilometres away.

As the lads were being dismissed at the end of the march, Alf Wiggins took Ted to one side and told him there was something of importance he wished to ask him.

"Major Crawford is concerned that we are losing so many NCOs, subsequently he's asked me to nominate men from the ranks who would be capable of replacing them. Now I've known you for a long time Ted, both before and during your military service, and I am of the firm opinion that your name should be at the top of the list." Clearing his throat, Alf then went on to say. "First of all you'd receive one stripe, in a couple of weeks another, then by the end of the month you'd be made up to full sergeant – rapid promotion I know, but don't forget it happened to me and you've got exactly the same length of service as I have."

For several moments, Ted was completely lost in thought, but eventually he asked for time to consider the matter.

"Well of course," replied the sergeant, "but don't leave it too long, Ted as we badly need more NCOs and we need them now."

**Officers of the Regiment**

# CHAPTER 6

## Over the Top

Withdrawn from the dreaded Ypres Salient, the 46th Division was replaced by the 17th Division, of which the 7th Lincolns were now such an essential part.

What a good job it was that each man had been issued with thigh-high waders, as heavy afternoon rain caused stinking knee-deep water to ebb and flow along the forward trench. Death and destruction blended with the dreadful stench of excrement and urine, which had spewed out of the far from perfect latrine, after a howitzer shell made a direct hit on it. God help anyone who may have been using it at the time. Rapidly becoming a health hazard, such wretchedness was merely accepted as being one of those annoying situations which so often occurred in war zones.

Newly promoted Sergeant John (Charlie) Cooper and two dozen lesser ranks, under the command of Lieutenant Hayward, were installed in the same trench as before, although they were now in Bay 12 instead of Bay 9. Some fresh faces had been drafted in, although Ted, Tom Weller, George Rush, Ted Paton, Arthur Skins, Bill Dobson and Jasper Houghton had been together since Lincoln racecourse days.

Not yet twenty-one years of age, Lieutenant Hayward was respected by all who served under him, for not unlike a few more of the younger officers he never asked his men to do anything which he wasn't prepared to do himself. Prior to commencement of hostilities, he was a renowned racing motorcyclist, often competing at such venues as Brooklands on his famous Douglas, known as Bumble Bee.

A sudden burst of rifle fire from enemy trenches was merely a warning to let Tommy know it was time to keep his head down, as neither side relished the thought of becoming involved in any form of heroics in such appalling weather conditions. In other words, if one side was experiencing huge problems, then so was the other.

It was virtually impossible to move field guns, and as horses couldn't stand upright, several had to be shot on the spot. This was a task which the lads found abhorrent, especially as many of them had spent much of their younger lives working alongside magnificent shires in the Lincolnshire countryside.

Slithering from firing platforms into the mire below, every saturated Tommy wished he could be anywhere other than where he was. Wood was too wet to get a fire started to make tea, and when bully and biscuits became too sodden to eat, everything became intolerable.

Everyone involved registered their bitter disapproval at the plight in which they found themselves. Some put the blame fairly and squarely on the shoulders of the generals, while others pointed the finger at Kitchener for having the impertinence to urge them to volunteer in the first place. There were others, of course, who were quick to accuse the German artillery boys of only being able to hit a makeshift latrine – or words to that effect. It was, however, Alf Letts who summed up the appalling situation best of all when he said, "what a bloody awful way to spend a Saturday night."

Holes which previous occupants had purposely dug into the trench sides to give some sort of refuge from mortar bombs were now so full of contaminated flood water they were of no use. Consequently, all the lads could do was grumble and Tommy being Tommy, my God could he grumble.

Within two days of the deluge terminating, the line was blessed with blue skies and sunshine, thus enabling totally exhausted infantrymen a short space of time to begin trench mopping-up operations. This, of course, didn't mean that the greatly improved atmospheric conditions would allow them ample time to recover from their distressing ordeal. In fact, if anything it was just the opposite.

Orchestrating the campaign from their holy of holies – GHQ – far away to the rear, those over-decorated, ostentatious military so-called experts, so often lampooned by Tommy as being 'faceless figures of fun' suddenly decided, in their misguided judgment, to stage an immediate 'over the top' attack in order to test enemy resolve.

Water-filled shell holes by the thousand, a sea of mud and razor-sharp barbed wire entanglements, combined with rapid retaliatory fire, rendered such an ill-conceived venture an utter disaster within thirty seconds of commencement. The outcome being death, bloodshed and complete humiliation. To make matters worse, stretcher-bearers became easy targets for Fritz's marksmen as they attempted to rescue the wounded.

Seeing what an impossible situation his troops were in, Major Crawford gave the order to retreat and almost at the same time, every other unit leader did likewise. The major was an extremely popular officer with his men, although they were all well aware that he didn't suffer fools lightly. Storming off down the trench, he bitterly condemned those brainless idiots at GHQ who'd given the order for such an attack to be carried out, and he didn't much care who heard him either. Neither did

Lieutenant Hayward make any secret of his contempt for the very same clowns who had so much influence over front-line tactics. In fact, his choice of language with which to vent his feelings was on a par with Tommy's, when passing an opinion on some particular bone of contention amongst the lads.

Not having heard the young OC use such inelegant speech before, Ted was somewhat aghast, yet at the same time he realised there was little to choose between Trench Tommy and Trench Officer when it came to expressing opinions on something that didn't suit. Meanwhile, Fritz must have thought that the 17th Division had either gone completely bonkers or that they'd all been on the bottle.

......................................

Contents of the well-stocked wine cellar at the imposing, admirably furnished chateau, which had been specifically requisitioned for the use of those supercilious high-ranking British officers, was in constant demand, as they relaxed in what was once the music room.

Congratulating themselves on giving 'old Jerry' a short sharp kick up the backside, it mattered not that their arrogance and incompetence had caused so much unnecessary heartache amongst loved ones back home in Blighty.

"My gad, sir… what… we're the important ones, you know," they so often repeated.

All of them were typical second in lineage progeny of the British aristocracy and because they had no chance of inheriting family estates and fortunes, their fathers had pushed them into accepting instant commissions, and in next to no time, they were shipped off to India or the like, where they spent a weird and wonderful existence

50

doing as little as possible, other than endeavouring to impress upon fellow officers and men, just how important they were. Nevertheless, mainly because of the old school-tie network, they were continually being promoted, though exactly what their rows of medal ribbons were for was anyone's guess.

Coming to the end of their unimpressive careers, they were posted to relatively undemanding positions at GHQ in France, which again meant promotion and even more medals.

Little wonder that Tommy and his front-line officers were so hostile towards a system which gave overriding control to a bunch of high-ranking individuals with no knowledge of modern warfare whatsoever. In fact, it was regarded as highly doubtful whether any of them had ever seen a trench, let alone a German soldier. It was, however, as Tommy so often remarked, "his old granny could do a bloody sight better job, blindfolded."

..........................................

Amidst the fear and despondency, a great many acts of sheer heroism emerged, but one which delighted Ted most of all happened as a stretcher-bearer successfully carried a wounded man into Bay 12, with a fusillade of Fritz's bullets miraculously missing him by a mere whisker.

It was Ted who held the stretcher-bearer's lower back to guide him down the trench ladder, but as he turned around, the pair of them suddenly cried out with joy, for it was no other than Humphrey Rudkin, Ted's great pal from Buckminster Hall Garden days.

Two other stretcher-bearers immediately attended the wounded man, while Ted and Humphrey shook hands and hugged each other like the great friends they so obviously were. Constantly talking about how their lives had irrevocably changed and how old friends and colleagues were getting along, each was able to acquaint the other with small detailed descriptions of happenings back in their village.

The chance encounter was only brief, but both agreed they'd do their utmost to contact each other as soon as 'B' Company received their relief.

# CHAPTER 7

## City of the Dead

Trench warfare, with its terrifying adversities, became a way of life for all infantrymen. Those unmistakable signs of youthful bravado having long since disappeared, leaving young men visibly aged well before their time.

Death, horrendous wounds, cries of the dying and damned, mass destruction, shellfire, mud, bullets, mortar bombs, ear-shattering noises, the ever-present stench, fear of the unknown, alongside the many blatant misjudgements of strategy, all contributed to the deterioration of morale and attitude. Mind over matter became matter over mind, as the perception of terror escalated.

By early September, the 7th Lincolns had been in and out of the trenches so often they were showing signs of fatigue, and, when they met up with other members of the 17th Division such as Sherwoods or South Staffs, they, too, openly complained about the attitude of those in the highest echelons of command. Influential bigwigs, whose absurd plans of action were responsible for so much unnecessary heartache.

..........................................

Rumours were widespread amongst all ranks that the most powerful politicians in London were becoming increasingly perturbed at the continuous deadlocked situation, in so far as no worthwhile advance had been made over the entire twelve-month period since hostilities commenced, and that it was only those unacceptable death-toll figures which continually made newspaper headlines. Proficient front-line officers were openly critical of the incompetent diehards at GHQ and eventually such expressions of discontent and frustration reached the ears of those who mattered most at the War Office.

Enthusiastic young men, who proudly accepted the King's shilling, did so with a strong belief that whatever was thrown at them by the enemy, they would, at the very least, be guaranteed genuine consideration and respect from their own leadership. Such expectation, however, was merely idealism and it didn't take long for the bona fide front-line fighting man to fathom out that those self-glorifying egotists only looked after themselves.

The relief billet just off the Zillebeke Road at Ypres was far from elaborate, but at least it was an improvement to the contaminated trenches, where death lurked day and night.

...........................................

Ted's very first close-up sighting of Ypres or Wipers, as Tommy preferred to call it, took place during one moonlit night when riding through its war-ravaged streets in an army limber. Both Arthur Brayshaw and Frank Gent were alongside him, as well as the driver, of course – their destination being a shell-damaged food store just off the Menin Road, where they were under orders to retrieve any worthwhile stock.

The trio of mates had seen pre-war picture postcards of the famous old city, but they were completely unprepared for the dreadful sight which greeted them close to where Belgium's finest buildings once stood – those being St Martin's Cathedral and the imposing Cloth Hall. To come across such horrifying destruction was a harrowing experience; no wonder it was referred to as the 'city of the dead,' for not one living soul, stray dog or cat was anywhere to be seen.

Entering the Grande Place, the shocking cataclysm worsened, as ruins stood out in hideous vividness. Was this the valley of the shadow of death which the three friends were witnessing at first hand, or was it a brief encounter with what the future held in store for civilisation? Or indeed, if mankind could commit such acts of unrestrained ferocity against each other, then would there even be a future?

During those few brief moments, Ted wondered if the human race had gone completely insane and he wished that all those who believed in the glorification of war could be made to ride along this main thoroughfare as he was now doing. If only the world's aggressors could see this dead city, with all its hideous examples of wilful destruction, then maybe, just maybe, the voice of conscience might stir their nefarious minds into exercising a great deal more caution.

Rattling along on what was left of the cobble-stoned roadway, the limber's wheels vibrated unharmoniously, but there was no one about to complain, only the four occupants whose emotionally disturbed minds clearly had other things to occupy them.

..........................................

The very last thing those three 'B' Company mates expected to be doing the following morning was to be marching along the very same route through Ypres centre as they'd taken in the limber.

All eyes stared unbelievably at the sheer devastation around them and not one single member of the battalion ventured to speak until new billets were reached at Vlamestinge, three kilometres away.

Occupying huts on a spot where the village once stood before enemy shells raised it to the ground, Tommy found them bare of any furnishings and rat-infested into the bargain. Outside, the real problem was the huge craters made by exploding howitzer shells, which had filled up with muddy water. Anyone slipping off the treacherous duckboards could very quickly sink into several feet of the brown stuff and once this occurred, there was no chance whatsoever of getting out alive.

Two days were spent dicing with death before the battalion was moved back to Ypres, this time to billets in the cellars of ruined shops, close to the city centre. Many men from different regiments were housed there and although they were well within the range of heavy German artillery, for the first time since setting foot on foreign soil, the lads enjoyed the luxury of being able to sleep in real beds with real mattresses and blankets. It mattered not that other Tommies before them had slept in those very same resting places and, judging by the colour of the sheets, with their boots on too!

The beds and furnishings were not provided courtesy of the British Army, but by those courageous citizens who had no further use of them after being on the receiving end of German artillery fire.

Ruins of the Cathedral and Cloth Hall. Ypres

The Cloth Hall, Ypres

# CHAPTER 8

## Just Two Young Boys

It soon became obvious that the larger than usual concentration of men in one place were not there for the good of their health, the significance being all too apparent. Rumour was still spreading among the battalions involved about a major assault having been predetermined and that it was supposedly scheduled to take place sooner, rather than later.

Far more enlightened than most, that ubiquitous brotherhood – the officers' servants – knew exactly what was likely to occur in the near future, for they were often performing their duties at GHQ, when top brass were formulating plans of action. Not that they had any desire to eavesdrop on conversations, but when those arrogant, self-infatuated, high-ranking old buffers were working at their huge round table, with a pencil in one hand and a large scotch in the other, the decibel measurement of conversation was considerably louder than normal.

Information gathered was, more often than not, passed onto drinking pals in the estaminets and in next to no time, the jungle telegraph alerted others to the possibility of forthcoming matters of interest.

On this particular occasion, it transpired that in August, Lord Kitchener had arrived in France to meet Sir John French, commander-in-chief (or C-in-C) of British troops, as well as General Joffre, the French counterpart, together with their respective cliques of egocentric advisers. Not that it took Kitchener too long to see through these so-called aides, for he wasn't a man to suffer fools lightly. Rapidly brought down to earth with a bump, they were reduced to the role of onlookers, and they squirmed uneasily, not unlike farmyard poultry when a hungry fox has entered their roost.

Influential parliamentarians back in Westminster, who possessed no experience of front-line fighting and all its implications, had obviously won the argument over battle tactics by demanding immediate success, to placate an increasingly sceptical press.

Joffre's plan, it seemed, was for the British to stage an all-out attack between Loos and La Bassee in early September, while French troops would simultaneously carry out a similar assault in the Champagne Region.

Once again, it was billet hearsay which suggested that plans for a combined offensive were not as straightforward as might have been, for it was common knowledge that French and Joffre were not the best of allies. For varying reasons, French made it perfectly clear that he was not in favour of an assault taking place on such a bare plain, but his protestations were apparently overruled by Kitchener, and the offensive was scheduled to take place during the first week of September.

On the 4th of the month, the 7th Lincolns returned to a line east of Sanctuary Wood, an area they knew only too well. Their orders were to create a diversion, by firing as many rapid rounds as possible, followed by keeping low-down for short intervals, then repeating the tactic. Supposedly, this was to be carried out in order to keep Fritz guessing, whereby he wouldn't suspect a high-priority attack was to take place elsewhere.

All hell was let loose as the artillery boys lambasted enemy lines, a stratagem which continued for two whole days, until information filtered through that the main offensive had been temporarily postponed.

For two weeks after this setback, the Lincolns kept their heads well down, the main reason being a shortage of ammunition, although a little matter like that didn't prevent the odd flare-up between the antagonists. In fact, it was during one of those tit-for-tat shindigs that Major Crawford received wounds which necessitated his hasty removal back to Blighty, thus making it necessary for a temporary restructuring amongst the chain of command.

..........................................

The Loos offensive was finally launched on the 25th September and, at first, splendid reports filtered through of its great success. The first German line was taken, quickly followed by the second; indeed, it appeared to be a marvellous victory.

Newspapers back in Blighty couldn't praise Kitchener enough as headlines such as 'A Great British Victory at Long Last,' were eagerly read in every town and village throughout the land. Unfortunately, however, what was imagined to be a huge success, turned out to be a great failure.

It was common knowledge amongst the troops that neither Sir Douglas Haig nor Sir John French favoured such an attack being carried out, as they both agreed that the terrain was unsuitable, as well as enemy defences being far too powerful to be effectively reduced by the inadequate strength of our own artillery at that particular time.

Their combined fears were very quickly justified and it soon became obvious that the whole ill-advised action was taken by Kitchener to pacify Joffre, as well as those interfering amateurs in Westminster.

..........................................

Two months of punishing rear-guard action, with only two short reliefs, saw the Lincolns, Sherwoods and Staffs, holding on to survive long periods of enemy artillery bombardment. Several old colleagues were killed, while many others lost limbs or sight, and in some instances, both.

Youngsters from training camps in the UK were being drafted in as replacements, although the flow of new arrivals decreased as time passed by.

Having fifteen months service behind him, the last five of them in and out of the line, Ted was now regarded as being an 'old sweat' and, not unlike the others he'd served with during that time, it seemed more like five years.

Lieutenant Hayward came marching down the trench and told Ted to look out for two replacements and to take them under his wing. Duly arriving, it was fairly obvious that neither of them had turned eighteen, although they were both trying to grow moustaches in an attempt to look older.

Introducing himself to the newcomers, Ted could tell they were pleased that, at last, someone was showing an interest in their wellbeing.

He advised the two of them that the golden rule amongst the lads in the trenches was to look after themselves at all times, and also their mates whenever possible. He also emphasised that they were not to try any heroics, or they wouldn't last the day out.

Within a couple of minutes of relating those significant words of wisdom, Fritz heavily bombarded the entire length of the Ypres Salient and Ted found himself pushing both boys into trench-side junk holes. British artillery retaliated in due course and the two boys covered their ears with both hands.

Next morning, the youngsters apologised to Ted for seemingly showing fear so easily, but he told them they had no need to apologise to anyone, as he'd never yet come across one single front-line Tommy who claimed not to be afraid when the going became really difficult.

Within the hour, Lieutenant Hayward sent for Ted and during his absence, Jerry dropped a mortar shell in the trench where the two boys stood talking, their deaths being instantaneous.

Returning to his post, Ted was extremely upset and for the first time in his life, he found himself questioning if there really was a God.

Well aware that on numerous occasions, he himself had narrowly missed death, but at that moment in time, those two extremely likeable boys hadn't even lasted twenty-four hours before their mutilated bodies were being carried away by stretcher bearers – and Ted didn't even know their names.

# CHAPTER 9

## The Royal Flying Corps

The 17th December 1915 was a date to be remembered, for not only was the 17th Division ordered to stand down, but also it was the very same day on which Sir John French was prevailed upon by the cabinet at Westminster to resign from his position as head of British armies in France and Belgium. Not that it came as any surprise to Tommy that Sir John was relieved of his command and neither did the appointment in his place of the ambitious Sir Douglas Haig.

.........................................

Scurrying away from the trenches, the 7th Lincolns ran helter-skelter through what remained of Sanctuary Wood, like panic-stricken rabbits escaping from a cornfield as horses and binder are three parts through harvesting it. Zigzagging across shell-cratered terrain, their immediate purpose being to attempt to stay in the land of the living.

How difficult it was for Tommy to imagine that this very same unsightly location was once a picturesque natural landscape, where wild flowers bloomed amongst blades of rich green grass that cattle chewed from dawn until dusk.

It would have been a place of serene beauty, where young lovers in search of forbidden fruits would wander without a care in the world. Now it was just something from a bygone age, of which the lads in khaki thought they'd never ever see the likes again.

'B' Company's new billet was in a group of old cottages close to the Menin Bridge, and by some miracle or other, they had barely been scarred by the ravages of war. It seems their occupiers moved away from them several years earlier, never to return.

The army labour force had made a reasonable job of renovating the cottages and both running water and a simple form of heating had been recently installed.

How wonderful it was to be able to do all those little important things in life which normal people in normal environments take for granted. Soaking feet in hot water was sheer bliss, but of course, only possible after cutting off blood-soaked boots and socks with a sharpened bayonet.

Trimming toenails and washing itchy scalps was absolute ecstasy, while taking a long exhilarating bath was almost too good to be true.

The call of nature awoke Ted early next morning. The cold unpleasant air was somehow different to anything he'd ever smelt before, being both sweet-scented and somewhat sickly. Shaking-off his half-slumber feeling, it suddenly dawned upon him that the obnoxious odour was gas, so realising the seriousness of the situation, he raced back along the recently modified corridor, awakening both officers and men to warn them of the imminent danger.

For quite some time, it was panic stations, as everyone in 'B' Company struggled to put on their gas helmets whilst at the same time battling to find uniforms and boots. Putting the wrong foot into a wrong trouser leg had the lads falling about and shouting obscenities like a Boston bull drover in a thunderstorm. Eventually, they were ordered outside by Lieutenant Hayward, and what a motley lot they looked.

At the time, it was thought that Jerry was flooding the Ypres region with gas prior to making a bold bid for the city. Thankfully, however, this was not so, as it soon transpired they had made an attack on the 6th Division's line, and a strong wind had carried the tail-end of it across the outskirts. It was the first time that General Plumer's 2nd Army had experienced a gas attack, and later it was confirmed that it claimed quite a number of casualties.

.........................................

As soon as the pandemonium calmed down, laughter broke out amongst the lads for they suddenly realised what a ragbag outfit they must have looked. Meanwhile the OC sent for Ted and thanked him for being so perceptive. Then, much to his amazement, he was asked to close the door and take a seat. He was even more astounded when the lieutenant poured out a couple of king-sized whiskies, and wished him the very best of health.

Trying his utmost to act in a normal way, Ted knew full well that officers didn't just happen to offer ordinary infantrymen a glass of whisky, so naturally he wondered what was coming next.

Not once looking towards Ted, the OC began to speak.

"I thought I'd just take this opportunity to tell you that I've become completely disillusioned with life in the trenches, as well as with the prize idiots at GHQ, who are responsible for front-line tactics and decisions."

There was rather a long pause, but Ted was now even more curious to find out why the lieutenant was taking time to discuss his discontentment with a mere private.

"You see, I'm a machine man at heart, and I desperately wish to become involved in aerial warfare, for I firmly believe that I can contribute far more to our country's cause by doing so."

Still slightly bemused at why his OC was telling him this, Ted nevertheless found himself thinking what a lucky so-and-so his officer was, especially when he went on to say that his application to transfer to the Royal Flying Corps had been accepted and that he'd be leaving 'B' Company within a few days.

Not really knowing what to say, Ted merely offered his congratulations and added that all the lads who'd served under him would miss him. It was then that Lieutenant Hayward dropped a real bombshell.

"I have noticed for quite some time that you possess all the qualities of a leader of men, yet twice to my knowledge you have refused promotion. I wonder, therefore, if I can persuade you to come along with me, as my servant?"

Persuade me, thought Ted, good God Almighty, of course I'd go with you, the sooner the better.

"Yes sir, I'd very much like the opportunity to go with you," he replied, quietly.

.....................................

Without needing time to deliberate over the offer, Ted knew it would be difficult to part from his mates, although many of them had already gone to meet their maker.

He thought if he didn't take this opportunity to get out now, then he too might well be joining them. He also reasoned that as he rarely saw the two Buckminster lads, with whom he enlisted, it was even more reason to grasp the chance being offered.

Thinking of how marvellous it would be to get away from the dreaded shellfire, the continuous ducking and diving from rifle bullets, the likelihood of being blown-up by mortar-bombs, the appalling noise and the constant smell of death and trench mud – who wouldn't exchange such conditions for a good clean bed every night.

Other little things which Ted had taken for granted suddenly flashed through his mind. Things like the notices written in blue crayon near Bay 9 dugout – 'Catchem Corner' and 'Hell-Fire Corner'. He also thought of those giant roots of a shell-battered tree which protruded into the trench, under which he sometimes managed to snatch forty winks. But most of all, he remembered the mutilated bodies of dead colleagues, who'd come over from Blighty in such high spirits but who would forever remain in some foreign field.

..........................................

Arrangements were speedily prepared for Ted to join Lieutenant Hayward and so on Christmas Eve 1915 the pair of them set out from Ypres to make their way to the Lincolnshire Regiment's transport depot at Reningelst. Christmas Day and Boxing Day were spent there, the lieutenant with an old friend of his, Lieutenant O'Farrel the transport officer, while Ted mucked-in with the officer's cook, Joe Pratt.

A professional chef before enlisting, Joe served up meals the like of which Ted hadn't seen or tasted since living at home as a teenager, with his parents in Market Harborough. What an unbelievable improvement it was compared with the insufficient, tasteless apology for food that the lads in 'B' Company were used to.

Saying their final goodbyes to the Lincolns, Lieutenant Hayward and Ted were driven to Poperinge where they boarded a train for St Omer, the officer, having to report to a Royal Flying Corps reception room, before continuing the journey to a squadron at Bailleul.

It was late evening before Ted dropped into bed in his very own more than adequately furnished room. Laying there he complimented himself upon making such an excellent move and he couldn't help but wonder how the lads on the Salient would envy him his new position.

There would be no more intolerable trenches, no more shells and bullets, no more striving to take the life of some mother's son, and as an added bonus, being able to take off boots and socks every night. What more could any man ask for?

Adapting quickly to their new lifestyles, both Ted and his officer were billeted in a large chateau just beyond the airfield boundary. Lieutenant Hayward lodged with five other officers on the first floor, while Ted and five other batmen occupied rooms on the ground floor.

As the lieutenant was undergoing a week's intensive aerial training, Ted spent much of his time assisting with officer's mess table-serving duties, for which it must be said, he considered himself totally unsuited. Nevertheless, he thought he could quite easily countenance such subservient tasks, especially as it guaranteed a decent night's sleep at the end of each day, with every facility on hand to keep him clean and free of those clinging companions which no trench Tommy is ever without.

As soon as Lieutenant Hayward had completed the course, Ted resumed full-time duties at the chateau, although he regarded it as being the most undemanding form of employment ever undertaken.

Accepted as a fully qualified observer air gunner after just one week's training, the lieutenant began to carry out reconnoitring sorties over enemy lines on an almost daily basis. Upon his return, Ted would take to him whatever requirements he'd requested and not once did he not ask Ted to pull up a chair and sit down. He very much liked to chat about things in general, as well as wanting to know if any news had been received from anyone in 'B' Company. Now and again, he would mention how sorry he'd been to leave such a splendid group of lads, even surprising Ted by his knowledge of almost every member's little idiosyncrasies.

Ted experienced great difficulty in believing that the five other servants slept in pyjamas, and he wondered what the lads in the trenches would have to say about such luxury – and didn't they do well for meals too, for it was almost like living in a high-class hotel. Everything needed was funded by the RFC, and only the best quality provisions were purchased from local shops – and to think that not too far distant, a war was in full swing, with Tommy having to survive on bully and hard biscuits. Here they enjoyed six-course dinners, commencing with oysters and finishing with coffee in the drawing room.

..........................................

On January the 17th, 1916, the sun had successfully broken through late morning cloud and Ted began to wonder why Lieutenant Hayward hadn't returned to the chateau. Later, his wondering turned to worry, for he was well aware that his officer was out on a reconnaissance operation over enemy lines.

News gradually began to circulate amongst the men that another of our aircraft was missing, the third morning in succession such a disaster had occurred.

Later still, it was confirmed that Lieutenant Watts and Lieutenant Hayward were the two officers involved.

The Germans reported the crash details via an arrangement adopted by both sides in the conflict and this verified that the Sopwith was shot down by a Fokker, killing both crew members. Both were young men – Lieutenant Hayward only just having reached his 21st birthday. Ted had known him from when they first enlisted. He trained under him at Bovington, crossed the Channel with him – a more popular officer with the lads would be difficult to find.

Not only was Ted aware that he'd lost a fine officer but also a real friend, an unusual bond considering the difference in rank. It was one more precious life cut short, one more sacrifice to add to the multitude who'd died doing their duty bravely. How thankful England should be, knowing she had bred such admirable sons.

Writing to Lieutenant Hayward's mother at 4 Mainwaring Road, Lincoln, Ted provided as many details of her son's death as possible, while at the same time letting her know exactly how much the lads of 'B' Company admired and respected him.

Beautifully written, her reply thanked Ted for all the kindness he'd shown towards her son, and asked him to convey the same sentiments to all 'B' Company members. As a battle-hardened front-line infantryman, life had taught Ted not to show his emotional feelings, but as he read and re-read the letter, tears of humility filled his eyes.

**Lieutenant C. O. Hayward**

7th Lincolnshire Regt. (attd. R.F.C.).
Complimented by his general for his
share in the fighting of December last

# KILLED IN ACTION.

HAYWARD.—On the 17th Jan., killed in Flanders, CHARLES
OSWALD HAYWARD, Lieut., 7th Lincolnshire Regiment, attached
Royal Flying Corps, the dearly-loved son of Mrs. H. C. Wilson
and the late Charles P. Hayward, of Beaumont Lodge, Lincoln,
aged 21 years.

..............................

# CHAPTER 10
## Back in the old Routine

Within twenty-four hours of Lieutenant Hayward's cruel death, Ted was summoned to attend an interview with a RFC personnel officer.

"Would you be prepared to transfer to the Royal Flying Corps on a permanent basis, although at the moment, a position of officer's servant is not readily available?"

Thinking of conditions in the RFC, with all the comforts of a pre-war home, as opposed to the hopelessness of life in the trenches, Ted's response was immediate and straight to the point.

"Yes, sir, ready and willing, sir"

"In that case, please state what experience you've had with aeroplane engines."

Well that really did put the cat amongst the pigeons.

"Er, aircraft engines sir? Er, no experience whatsoever sir…"

The interview was terminated for the time being, but next morning Ted received a message from the very same officer telling him to parade at the orderly room, with full kit and belongings at 3pm prompt, in order to rejoin his regiment.

How pleased Ted was to find out the 7th Lincolns were 'at rest' in the St Omer district. First of all it was a thirty-kilometre train journey, followed by a seven-kilometre walk to a village by the name of Eperlecques, where 'B' Company was tracked down at a large farm.

The first man Ted bumped into was Alf Wiggins and how pleased they both were to see each other. Several more old mates came and shook hands and told him how delighted they were to see that he'd decided to desert the Flying Corps and return to the pleasures of life in the trenches.

Informing the lads of Lieutenant Hayward's death saw them all deeply saddened, which was testimony to the great esteem in which he was held.

On parade next morning, both Captain Metcalfe, the deputy CO of the Brigade and Lieutenant Treddenick, the new OC of 'B' Company asked Ted to fall out, as being good friends of Lieutenant Hayward, they wished to know full details regarding his death.

........................................

Delighted to be back with such a great bunch of lads, Ted promised himself that never again would he defect to the Royal Flying Corps, or to anywhere else for that matter.

Sleeping on straw, in the larger of the two barns adjacent to the farmhouse, the entire company seemed to be quite content with their present situation. Both the farmer and his wife were genuinely kind people, often inviting the lads inside for coffee, homemade biscuits and a friendly chat. How nice it was to be given such a warm welcome and to be asked to sit in comfortable armchairs in a real lived-in house.

The couple's two charming daughters were great favourites of the younger Tommies – no doubt reminding them of girlfriends they'd left behind in Blighty. Also, many friendships were made in the village, the inhabitants treating the lads exceptionally well.

Unfortunately, all good things must come to an end, so as the rest period expired, the battalion came together at St Omer railhead from where they travelled to Godewaersvelds. It was then a march to the village of Deklijet via Renimghelst, where they were to occupy dilapidated Belgian army huts.

During the night the heavens opened turning well-worn ground outside into a virtual mud trap. Wondering what he could come up with to keep the men occupied, Captain Metcalfe hastily decided that a kit inspection should take place at 9am, inside each individual hut. Tommy, naturally, absolutely detested such meaningless rituals and each and every one of them was on tenterhooks.

No one in any regiment in the British army derived any pleasure from kit inspections, as more often than not, a sizeable proportion of the lads ended up being 'up for orders'.

The golden rule was that Tommy should, at all times, have in his possession that which had been issued to him – this hard-and-fast ruling being reiterated from day one of his service. But Tommy being Tommy this was rarely the case.

Captain Metcalfe followed obediently by his second in command, the adjutant, the OC, the Lieutenant Quartermaster, the Quartermaster Sergeant, the RSM, the CSM and two corporals, all with faces like stone gargoyles, marched into 'B' Company's hut.

First stop was at the end of Bill Dobson's so-called bed. The CO then turning towards the CSM shouted, "I say, Sergeant Major, this man's towel is an absolute disgrace. Why is that?"

"I would imagine he hasn't bothered to wash it, sir."

Turning and facing a sheepish looking Dobson, the CO said, "Right then, I want that washed and dried within the hour. Don't you realise you could grow a hundred weight of swedes in all that mud?"

"Where are your iron rations, Letts?"

"I haven't got any, sir."

"I say did you hear that, Quartermaster? Hasn't he been issued with any?"

"Yes, sir, every man, sir."

"Take his name, sergeant."

Picking up a half-hidden empty bully-beef can, with the end of his cane, the CO called to the offender, "I say, Weller, where's the bully disappeared to?"

"I think the rats must have taken it, sir, when we were in the line, sir."

"Were you aware that rats could cut such a straight line with their teeth, Sergeant Major?"

"No, sir."

"Take his name."

"Yes, sir."

"I say, Quartermaster, this man's only showing one pair of socks, and they're on his feet. Where are your other two pairs, Keeble?"

"I must have mislaid them, sir."

"Mislaid them, man! How in God's name do you expect us to win the war if you've mislaid your socks?"

Several more lads were admonished for failing to display certain items which were Army property – and this being the British Army, it was considered a serious offence.

Finally, the inspection party moved off and each member of 'B' Company breathed a huge sigh of relief. That was, of course, apart from those who were caught out and they cursed the entire entourage with every ribald representation in their vocabularies. Tommy being Tommy, his repertoire of obscenities was quite extensive. Less than five minutes later the CSM returned.

"Right, you lot, do yer want the good news first or the bad?"

Immediately a chorus of voices piped up. "You may as well give us the good news first, sergeant major."

"Right then, thirty-one of you are being put on a 'fizzer' for disregarding military rules and regulations."

"I thought you said that's the good news, Sergeant Major," said one of the wrongdoers.

"Well, it is the good news considering that Captain Metcalfe has decided, in his wisdom, that under the circumstances the charges would be rescinded."

"So what circumstances would they be, sergeant major?"

"The circumstances being, that you'll all be back in the trenches within the next forty-eight hours." Suddenly there was a chorus of booing.

# CHAPTER 11

## Minenwerfer

Leaving the turbulent life of a front-line infantryman to take up the comparatively undemanding role of officer's servant in the Royal Flying Corps, Ted really did believe he'd seen the last of trench warfare, but fate and the gods decreed otherwise.

Barely a month had slipped by before he was back in the brainless business of armed conflict, together with quite a few of those marvellous colleagues, with whom he'd shared heartache and misery, sometimes almost to the point of despair.

Marching away from their Deklijet billets, the 7th Lincolns were allowed a few hours respite on the outskirts of Ypres, before continuing through the city centre and out again on the Westhoek Road. In semi-darkness they proceeded cautiously across the shell-pocked terrain, eventually slipping into the line, like partridges protecting their chicks from the hovering kestrel. The area they entered was known as 'The Bluff' and was a position of considerable tactical importance as an observation point.

Posted to sentry lookout, Ted occasionally fired his rifle in the general direction of enemy lines. Although he wasn't able to see anything worthwhile to shoot at, it merely served to let Fritz know he was still under surveillance. Now and again the Germans would retaliate, yet both sides artillery remained unusually quiet.

Not unlike their British adversaries, Jerry may also have suffered a temporary shortage of ammunition, and

Tommy certainly hoped this was so. Deep down, however, he couldn't help feeling this may very well be the lull before the storm, and in any case, at no time could he afford to be complacent.

On the third day of entering the line, Sergeant Wiggins selected a corporal and three privates to keep a watchful eye on a bridge, some five hundred metres or so behind the trenches. It seems it was strategically important, being on one of the main routes to and from the battle area. The Germans knew of its significance, as on numerous occasions they'd tried to blast it off the face of the earth.

Corporal Arthur Taylor, Frank Gent, Jack Cooper and Ted were well aware they'd fallen for a cushy number, as all they were required to do was prevent more than half a dozen men crossing the bridge at any one time, this being due to its defective condition. Previous guards had made themselves reasonably comfortable, having made a more than useful dugout beneath a high bank of earth, thirty metres downstream from the actual structure.

Congratulating themselves upon being given such an uncomplicated task, the foursome spent most of the first twenty-four hours making tea. But not unlike all fit, able-bodied young men, they began to feel in need of something a little more nourishing than bully and biscuits.

Not more than three kilometres away, in the valley to their left was a well-known military rations depot, to which army vehicles made night-time deliveries and quite close to it stood a large abandoned chateau, known to Tommy as Bedford House.

Agreeing amongst themselves that no one was likely to drop by to see if the four would-be connoisseurs of good cuisine were carrying out their duties like good competent soldiers, it was decided that the three privates would carry out a reconnaissance of the two buildings, and if at all possible, try and gain access in the hope of securing food as well as something to cook it with.

Sausage, bacon, eggs, beans, bread, butter and strawberry jam were pillaged from the depot, while Ted's ill-gotten gains included a large frying-pan and saucepan, as well as proper plates and cutlery, all washed in the brook near the bridge. What a meal Arthur Taylor cooked that night and there was so much of it that when Sergeant Alf Wiggins made a dawn visit to see if everything was satisfactory, he too enjoyed the same feast.

Huddled comfortably around the dying embers, spinning tales as only Tommy could, the relaxed atmosphere was suddenly brought to an abrupt halt, when rapid mortar fire opened up, followed by several almighty explosions which not only shook the earth violently, but also sent the five pals flying through the air like rag dolls.

Desperately trying to scramble to their feet, three more thunder-like blasts followed in quick succession. These were thought to be minenwerfers, and they were certainly too close for comfort.

Within a matter of seconds, all hell was let loose as both sides opened with heavy artillery, making the hideous, unbelievable noise unbearable. To add to the turmoil, there was the spiteful crack of rapid rifle fire as well as cascading coloured flashes of light, which fell from the heavens like innumerable fragments of lightning.

The helpless quintet wondered what in God's name was happening. Had British troops begun a raid or was Fritz attacking our lines in force? Or then again, were they witnessing the beginning of Armageddon?

Realising it was far more serious than a normal raiding party, the lads were in a real quandary as to know exactly what to do, but when enemy artillery dropped a 'heavy' on the bridge, which they were supposed to be guarding, the decision was made for them. Thankfully, not one missile landed on or near their temporary sanctuary, otherwise five more Lincolns would have been removed from the ration list.

Deciding to make their way as near as possible to their own section of the line, they not only came across complete devastation, but also many groups of men from different regiments running around aimlessly like petrified pigs in an abattoir when the slaughter-man makes his grand entrance – and my God were they justified in doing so.

After some form of stability was restored, it was confirmed that Fritz had detonated three huge minenwerfer, which had caused the utter confusion and disorder. Men had been thrown perilously through the air, putting a great many lives in jeopardy. Numerous others were killed instantly, while others were buried alive never to be seen again.

By the time the five lads met up with the 7th, they were in support of the 10th Sherwoods and 8th South Staffs, slightly north of the Ypres-Comines Canal, where they were held up while awaiting orders to take part in an assault on the steep wooded rise on the landscape, which was known by the British as 'The Bluff'. It was close to where they were situated before commencing their bridge-guarding duties, but because of minenwerfer and heavy artillery from both sides, the terrain deteriorated almost beyond recognition.

Extremely heavy fighting was taking place but superior German artillery was making life decidedly difficult for the three battalions involved, although the 10th Lancashire Fusiliers held the defences close to the north bank for quite some time.

It was fairly obvious to all concerned that the enemy had made The Bluff a high-priority venture. Subsequently, great numbers of their infantrymen were able to take their objective on the 14th February 1916.

The Lincolns who'd held their position for a whole day were forced into retreating against overwhelming odds, and rather than risk more casualties, HQ ordered them to retreat to billets at Reninhgelst.

Rear-guard action was still continuing the following day and the bombing units had even made it possible for 'D' Company Lincolns, who were attached to the 8th South Staffs, to launch a counter-attack.

The Bombers, who were commanded by 2nd Lieutenant Harold Hall, had carried out a marvellous job, though unfortunately the highly respected officer and several of his men were killed.

Back in Reninghelst, all returning officers and NCO's were visiting each individual billet in an effort to carry out a roll-call, to find out which men were still in the land of the living. Ted was keen to know if any more 'B' Company lads had made it back, but it came as a considerable shock to be told that John Hempsall, one of the Saddle-Room gang, was killed in the last day's action.

An extremely popular young man, John was only twenty-one. He came from the village of Normanton-on-Cliffe near Grantham, and left a young wife to face a rather bleak future.

**Sgt Alf Wiggins**
**Later CSM then Lieutenant**

– Good friend and a real gentleman –

# CHAPTER 12

## The Bluff Retaken

No one who'd spent those last two weeks of February 1916, in the small Belgium town of Reninghelst, ten kilometres south-west of Ypres, could fail to see that something out of the ordinary was about to take place. Highly effective manoeuvres were carried out on a daily basis and when the 7th Lincolns were joined by the 10th Sherwoods, as well as the 76th Brigade, some extremely serious trench-taking exercises were put into practice.

Although the 7th had only taken part in one serious 'over-the-top' assault on enemy lines, that was the fool's errand organised by those self-opinionated halfwits at GHQ, and that was only for want of something better to do.

Now they had been specially chosen to participate in a major offensive – the object being to retake 'The Bluff' at all costs.

On the night before the actual attack was due to take place, the entire camp was buzzing like a swarm of bees on a hot summer's day, for everyone was aware that he was to take part in something extra special.

Most of the lads had spent several months under bombardment in the trenches, and although many of their comrades had been killed or wounded, this was something of an unknown quantity and they all knew their courage and nerve would be tested to the limit. Though for the time being, they all laughed and joked, as if it was going to be plain sailing all the way.

It was not in the British nature to accept they had been outclassed in battle, but like any boxer worth his salt who had been defeated in the ring, Tommy wanted revenge.

The day of destiny finally arrived, and all troops, irrespective of rank, were on parade to receive final instructions, as well as extra ammunition and rations. Normally, Tommy carried one hundred and twenty rounds, but today he received two additional bandoliers to sling around his shoulders, along with, his usual issue of Mills bombs.

Marching towards the front-line, the battalions were purposely split into platoons in case of aerial observation or shelling of tracks. Passing large clusters of heavy guns, gave the lads a great stimulus knowing they had the mighty power of artillery to support them. Huge quantities of shells were stockpiled close by, awaiting the order to be despatched further ahead, while the Trench Mortar Batteries were hard at work pushing their deadly weapons in determined fashion towards the point of no return.

Just beyond Ypres, a long rest was taken, with soup wagons and coffee vans in attendance. As the late evening visibility gradually faded, there was a ban on smoking, as well as talking. Each man had his own private thoughts to contend with, for every single one of them was fully aware they'd be extremely fortunate to be walking back along the very same route in a few days' time.

Ted had his own thoughts and trepidations too. Was this to be the end? He asked himself. Was he marching towards his own execution? Nevermore than at that particular moment in time did he realise just how precious life was.

Stumbling along in the darkness, each individual platoon reached their assigned trench by midnight, which meant they could try and grab a few hours' sleep, although they knew this would be virtually impossible, with the occasional shell bursting around them.

The storm finally broke at 4.20am on the 2nd March. Ted had no idea how long he'd leaned against the side of the trench, or whether he'd been able to snatch any sleep, although he did remember shaking hands with Frank Gent as they wished each other the very best of luck. Hell had suddenly released all its fiends at the very same split second.

British guns opened up, creating one tremendous long roll of thunder, which continued for what seemed like an eternity, and a vivid spectrum of colour lit up the early morning sky as Fritz retaliated.

The noise was incessant, with heavies dropping all over the place. Flying shrapnel was causing pandemonium amongst advancing troops with the Highlanders taking the brunt of it, having left their forward position first.

Men of each regiment were dropping like swatted flies, until it became sheer butchery, with each individual fighting like someone possessed by the devil.

It was the longest insane day imaginable, with those who'd managed to evade the bullet, shouting and bayonet-charging like demented ogres.

When the surviving Lincolns regrouped in the first line as instructed, they needed to clamber over the dead and dying to do so. Men with limbs shot off were pleading for help, their faces and uniforms completely unrecognisable. It was all too frightful to wish them to live, and the expiration of life for which they begged, would come as a happy release from their agonies. Men who, less than a day earlier, were still in the full vigour of youth, now lay hideously misshapen in Flanders mud.

In the cold early morning air, a recent addition to 'B' Company, 2nd Lieutenant Shankster was in conversation with Corporal Hemsall and Ted, as they glanced over the trench parapet to survey the heinous sight ahead. Maybe they were half hoping that the terrible carnage they'd witnessed at first hand on the previous day was really just a gruesome nightmare, and that all the evidence had been effaced from the landscape by some all-powerful nocturnal magician.

Amongst the dead and dying, stretcher-bearers were out searching for signs of life in the most dreadful conditions imaginable. What magnificent exploits these unsung heroes undertook as they not only had to withstand the elements but also the snipers bullet.

Little more than forty metres distant, Ted noticed a slight movement from a horizontal Tommy who, in his terrifying situation, was still attempting to reach a place of sanctuary – just how long he must have suffered.

Disobeying the rule book and regardless of his own safety, Lieutenant Shankster leapt over the parapet, before very politely asking Corporal Hempsall and Ted if they would join him on his mission of mercy. Spasmodic rifle fire from the distant enemy marksman made the operation somewhat hazardous, but within a reasonable time, the trio carefully lifted the man – a King's Own lance corporal – and disregarding his screams, soon had him back in the trench. It was only then they noticed one of his legs was missing.

Racing off to find a stretcher-bearer, Ted was absolutely staggered to discover that the very first one he came across, was no other than his great pre-war pal Humphrey Rudkin from Buckminster. How the pair of them would have loved to stop for a good old chinwag, but the King's Own lad was in urgent need of expert treatment.

Surviving remnants of the three regiments involved in the first-wave assault were a little surprised at not being ordered to resume the attack. Trench-to-trench rifle fire had almost ceased, but a solitary shell came out of the blue, landing within a few feet of the lieutenant's dug-out.

Escaping with minor abrasions, the officer and Ted found themselves upside down in the trench bottom. Unfortunately, Corporal Fred Hempsall wasn't so fortunate and he was badly wounded.

When collecting the injured NCO, the two stretcher-bearers involved asked to speak to Ted, as they said they needed to talk to him about Humphrey Rudkin. It transpired he had also been seriously injured and was asking for Ted. Obviously, under the circumstances, it was impossible to obtain any form of release from duty at that particular moment in time, although he promised to call and see him as soon as they were relieved.

News gradually filtered down the line that Jerry had retreated and so officially The Bluff was recaptured – but at what a dreadful price.

In excess of a hundred German infantrymen came across no-mans-land with hands raised high, their officer holding a white flag to indicate they wished to surrender.

Under interrogation, it transpired that none of them had eaten for almost three days and they confirmed that a great many of their comrades were dead or horribly injured. Overnight frost and snow showers blew in on a westerly, making their position intolerable.

Survivors of the Gordons and King's Own, as well as the 7th Lincolns were also cold and hungry, but the word 'retreat' was no longer in their vocabulary.

Relief troops eventually arrived to strengthen the regained lines and those men who'd come through the conflict unscathed, stumbled over the dead bodies of both German and British troopers, in the hope of reaching billets before shelling recommenced.

Arriving at the new rest camp at De Klite, the 7th Battalion were given hot tea, well laced with rum and as much food as they could eat. Their final order was to get beneath blankets and remain there for the next twelve hours.

Stirring from their longer than usual slumber, the following morning, the animated conversations of the previous night were by now somewhat subdued, as each man was eager to find out what might have happened to their good mates.

Ted was unable to trace Frank Gent, and it came as a great shock to learn that he'd been killed within seconds of 'going over the top'.

Later still Ted found out that another good mate, Arthur Brayshaw, had also made the ultimate sacrifice. Aged twenty-six, Arthur was a Chester lad, and not unlike Frank, was a very popular member of the Saddle-Room gang.

# CHAPTER 13

## Goodbye Friend

There was no feeling of disappointment when the battalion learned they were being withdrawn from the dreaded Ypres Sector. From the moment they first entered Belgium in July of the previous year, up to late March 1916, the lads had absorbed their fair share of horror associated with the north European battleground.

Close trench fighting, bursting shells and glorious mud, was not recommended for physical well-being or mental equilibrium at the best of times, but with the worst of elements also to contend with, discharge of duty was even more demanding.

It was hoped the fresh billets at Bailleul might be a considerable improvement on those which the battalion were previously allocated, but upon arrival, their hopes were dashed when they were directed to a farm with the all-too-familiar straw beds in ramshackle barns.

Every garment needed to be washed or cleaned, while each and every man was given the 'short back and sides' treatment, as once again they were expected to look like well-disciplined soldiers of the King.

On the 7th day in Bailleul, 2nd Lieutenant Shankster sent for Ted, and it came as no surprise when he asked him if he would be kind enough to consider becoming his batman. How could he possibly refuse the request of such a polite man, so without giving it a second thought, his answer was in the affirmative. Ted knew it wouldn't keep him out of the line, but at least it would prevent him from attending so many parades, kit-inspections and the like.

The lieutenant's billet was in the loft of an old barn that had been specially converted to accommodate the military, while Ted was allocated a small room on the ground floor. Both were sparsely furnished, but at least they did have beds of a kind to sleep in, unlike 'B' Company who had to make do with straw scattered across the larger adjoining barn floor.

Ted had great difficulty in believing just how polite and thoughtful his new officer was, for not once did he fail to say please and thank you, however small a request he made.

Putting into practice some skilful negotiation technique, to secure a private billet for both himself and Lieutenant Parsloe in the actual farmhouse, two days later the two officers were able to come to an agreement with the farmer and his wife allowing Ted and Arthur Skins – Lieutenant Parsloe's batman – to use a former ground-floor store room.

Although quite elderly, the French couple were extremely kind and provided both Ted and Arthur with old mattresses to sleep on, and they also woke them up in the mornings with welcome cups of tea.

......................................

With the Battalion's rest period over, their turn for further trench warfare was fast approaching. This time, it was to be in the Armentières Sector, to which, they were informed, men were despatched to recuperate after undergoing turbulent times elsewhere.

How the lads loved those rests in French villages and towns, far away from the madhouse conditions of the front line. The residents never failed to make them extremely welcome, and subsequently many friendships were forged.

A ten-kilometre march took place to Armentières, where everyday business appeared to carry on as normal, in spite of it being no more than four kilometres from the line. The town was full of British troops, but amazingly the Germans didn't shell the place. The reason for this was an agreement reached by both sides which more or less guaranteed the British would not shell Lille, where a great many enemy troops were billeted, providing Jerry refrained from shelling Armentières.

Hoping satisfactory billets would be made available, the Lincolnshire lads were delighted when directed to a spacious nunnery, occupied only by a small group of nuns. Officers were allocated one of the larger first-floor rooms as a mess, with each of them having their personal quarters in cell-like rooms, close by. On the other hand, Tommy did as Tommy always did; he just dropped down wherever convenient in any of the disused ground-floor outer rooms.

Convinced that at long last their luck had changed for the better, the lads strolled through the town during the evenings, seemingly without a care in the world. As always, however, just as Tommy was enjoying a relaxed atmosphere, some joker came along and screwed everything up.

Orders came through for the 7th to take up positions at the front. What a contrast the new trenches were to those left behind in the Ypres Sector. Well duck-boarded, dry and clean, but maybe not quite up to the standard as delineated by some veterans when referring to them as being like a 'home from home'.

Shells of any description were rarely exchanged, so comparative calm remained for long periods at a time. Some strafing was actually carried out, during the cover of darkness, by a lone German machine-gunner, which earned him the nickname of 'parapet Joe', not that he ever hit anyone; then again, maybe he wasn't even trying to.

Supply lines were far more efficient to those on the Ypres Salient. Subsequently, there was always an ample supply of clean drinking water available.

Running all the way from Armentières to the Line was a communication trench, which not only made it easy to get ammunition and rations through, but if any of the officers needed extra supplies of alcoholic spirits, their servants would stroll the short distance from trench to shops and collect them, also purchasing cigarettes and tobacco for the lads, naturally!

Cutting through the forward trench was the officer's mess, an artistically created structure, which may well have been elaborately designed by Edwin Lutyens himself, it was that stylish. Boasting a shell-proof roof, tables, chairs, beds, other small furnishings and even carpets and curtains, little wonder it was such an attraction. Playing all the latest dance music, the gramophone was at times so loud, the lads reckoned they could see Fritz holding tea dances in his trench.

Other Company officers often paid a visit. Playing cards were brought out together with a comprehensive selection of booze and cigars, and afterwards, batmen would serve up five-course meals. What a totally different world it all seemed – it felt like playing at soldiers almost after previous terrifying experiences the battalion had gone through.

After only seven days at the front, the so-called 'active duty' period expired, and it was back to new billets although still in Armentières. 'B' Company took up residence in railway sheds close to the inoperative station, while officers made themselves at home in the nearby Station Hotel.

Off duty Tommy thoroughly enjoyed himself, and why not, for God knows he'd earned it. He liked his beer, his cigarettes, his sing-songs in the estaminets, and, of course, he especially enjoyed the company of those beautiful mademoiselles.

It was while billeted in Armentières, that Ted received the distressing news of Humphrey's death. It certainly came as a tremendous shock, as just over two weeks earlier, he'd been given to understand that his great friend of pre-war days was making a fine recovery from his wounds and was looking forward to an early return to Blighty.

Laying on his apology of a bed, Ted thought of all those happy times when Humphrey, Tom and he were at Buckminster. He thought of the football and cricket matches in which they'd taken part, and naturally he also thought of the morning the three of them rode their bicycles to Grantham to enlist.

The 9th April 1916 would forever remain in Ted's memory. For the time being, however, he was extremely emotionally distressed, for not only had he lost a real friend at the age of just twenty-four, but a very brave one as well.

Drummer W. H. RUDKIN (Lincolnshire Regiment), of Sproxton.

Another of our brave lads has fallen in action, news of which has just reached his grandmother, Mrs. Birch, sen., of Sproxton. Drummer W. H. Rudkin volunteered into the Lincolnshire Regiment, and received his training at Lulworth Camp, Dorset. He left England on the 14th of last July, and had seen a great deal of fighting. He came home on nine days' leave in February, in the best of health and spirits. He had returned to the front only a few days when he was wounded. Drummer Rudkin was engaged in stretcher-bearing work, and was helping to carry a wounded comrade when he was shot in both legs. His comrades expressed their high admiration of his pluck and bravery. They said he had done splendid work, and everyone was proud of him. Writing home to his grandmother, he said: "Dear grandmother,—I have got a 'blighty,' just enough to to bring me home to dear old England." Later, an official notification from the War Office stated that he had undergone an operation, and was seriously ill. Several letters have been received from one of the sisters at the hospital, in which she spoke of him as one of the best patients, and that everything possible would be done for him. On Wednesday last the sad news came he had died of wounds. Drummer Rudkin and his brother, who is also in the Army, were left orphans in 1902. They made their home with their grandmother, the widow of Mr. Robert Birch, for whom the deepest sympathy is felt. Previous to joining the Army, he was in the employ of Lord Dysart, Buckminster, as a gardener, for six years. The service last Sunday morning at Sproxton Church, was of an impressive character. The Vicar (Rev. H. B. Vale), in his address, made most touching reference to the gloom prevailing throughout the parish at the loss of one of our heroes. For some years Drummer Rudkin was a Church chorister. The hymn, "Peace, perfect peace," was sung, and at the close the "Dead March" in "Saul" was played.

94

**Humphrey was laid to rest at Etaples Military Cemetery**

# CHAPTER 14

# Eperlecques Interlude

Considering there was a war on, life in Armentières was totally different to what anyone in the 7th Lincolns had anticipated. From the officers in their luxury quarters to the boys in their comfortable billets, everyone was satisfied with conditions there.

Townsfolk seemed almost oblivious to the reality of what was taking place in other sectors, and the tit-for-tat, 'handbags-at-dawn' affray, just a mere stone's throw away, was so obviously designed by gentleman's agreement.

Given the choice, each member of every regiment stationed in Armentières would have elected to remain in the place for the duration, but of course the British Army isn't quite so accommodating, and so after a couple more eight-day spells in the Line, orders were posted for the entire battalion to move out at 9am, one sunny Sunday morning in May.

Neither officers nor men wished to leave their idyllic lifestyles, so in order to pay tribute to their admirable French friends, the night before departure day became one long celebration. Every estaminet in the town centre was packed to the rafters, alive with singing and laughter, as well as the customary giggles and sighs of those flirtatious mademoiselles.

The generous-natured French people were at times almost too good to be true. Singing along and shaking hands with their khaki-clad friends, they continually insisted they have just one more for the road, and of course, Tommy being Tommy, he had no idea how to refuse.

Because of the sorry condition of almost the entire battalion when morning roll was called, the CO Lieutenant Colonel Forrest read the riot act, telling all the lads they were a disgrace to the uniform they wore. He then delayed departure for a further six hours to allow them to recover their savoir-faire. Yet as the lads said afterwards, "The old boy didn't look any too clever himself", so maybe he also needed to get his head down just that little bit longer!

At precisely 2pm, the battalion paraded in the town centre, all ready to commence their marathon march to fresh billets, where it was understood they'd undergo rigorous battle training. Only at the very last minute were they informed a seventy-kilometre foot slog lay ahead of them, as their destination was to be Eperlecques, beyond St Omer. This seemed to cheer up the lads quite a bit, as this was the place they all knew well. But even so, the lads groaned, "Who needs a seventy-kilometre march, after a night like that!".

Taking more than three days to complete the journey, several men had to drop out en route, mainly because of sore feet. This meant they had to sit by the wayside and hopefully scrounge a lift with a passing army vehicle.

Being in motorised transport, Lieutenants' Shankster and Parsloe arrived in Eperlecques a couple of days earlier and they were already installed in a private house close to the village centre when Ted and Arthur Skins caught up with them.

The battalion was informed that they were shortly to take part in the greatest battle in the history of mankind, although for the time being, it was to be training, training and more training, until such time as they would become heartily sick of it. In a nutshell, Tommy was to practise the art of killing as many of the enemy as possible, before being killed himself.

Still it wasn't all work and no play, as the officer in charge of battle tactics realised the men would be more conducive to his training methods, if they were occasionally given something else to occupy their minds. Subsequently, senior NCOs were instructed to organise a football competition between the regimental companies involved in the programme.

For almost a whole month, intensive manoeuvres took precedence over everything else, although the football contest caused great interest. Ted's team, 'B' Company 7th Lincolns, did quite well but were eliminated at the semi-final stage, which left a Sherwoods' Company to play a Staffs' Company in the final on the last Saturday of the month. Unfortunately, when the great day arrived, there was a tremendous thunderstorm which caused the match to be postponed, rescheduled to take place the following day. Everything seemed to be going according to plan, until the padre objected, and so the game was never played.

On the very same evening, prior to the different battalions moving out next day, all men were ordered to attend church parade and what a mockery this turned out to be.

In the open air, on the makeshift parade ground, the padre preached his sermon, although not always in keeping with the principles of the Christian faith. In fact, any eavesdropper may well have been forgiven for thinking the entire charade was purposely arranged by the military authorities on the eve of battle, especially to incite Tommy into fulfilling his role with a far greater determination than ever before.

For all those in the gathering who'd witnessed at first hand the shootings, bombings, shellings, the aftermath of bayonet charging, men screaming in agony, having lost limbs or sight or with intestines lying in the mud, the padre's words were hypocritical. And to think, one of the commandments was – "Thou shall not kill."

Apparently, the padre believed it was quite in order for men to kill and be killed on the Sabbath, but my God, don't be caught kicking a football on a Sunday, as that really would upset the Almighty.

# CHAPTER 15

## Battle of The Somme

Irrespective of the punishing training schedule, everyone agreed what a delightful time was spent in Eperleques. Yet again, local hospitality was exceptional, with excellent hosts frequently inviting Tommy into their homes. As usual, the estaminets did a roaring trade, but considering just how many men were stationed in and around the village, not a single instance of trouble was reported.

Old hands were well aware they were training hard for something out of the ordinary, but to the young reinforcements fresh from Blighty, it still seemed like one big adventure. What bliss to be in ignorance of what lay ahead.

Almost every household turned out to wish the lads bon voyage, for they knew in their hearts this would be the last time they'd meet. Many of the old folk had tears in their eyes, and if the truth was known, so too did Tommy.

Beginning their journey with a ten-kilometre march to Audruicq followed by one of those never-ending monotonous cattle truck rides to Amiens, they eventually finished up at a village by the name of Allonville. Here, the 17th Division occupied several farm buildings, which were characteristically French. A week there, then a move was made to Heilly, close by the Ancre River, where a couple of nights were spent under canvas.

......................................

During the early hours of Saturday, July 1st 1916, the thunder-like roll of artillery fire signalled the beginning of the Battle of the Somme.

Crossing the Ancre, the battalion passed through Morlancourt and Méaulte, before taking up positions close to Fricourt, which was situated a short distance to the south-east of Albert. Here, they were instructed to stay put overnight, as it transpired the plan of action was for the artillery to bombard Fricourt Wood, as well as the open plain leading up to it, prior to the infantry making an all-out assault at daybreak. Meanwhile, the other battalions in the 17th were on the move slightly north of the Lincolns, with the intention of converging on Fricourt village from three sides.

The night was rather humid and the lads endeavoured to snatch whatever sleep they could in dried-out ditches, but once the heavies opened just before dawn, it took them all of their time to think clearly, let alone stir the creativity of over imaginative nightmares.

It was in this devilish spot when Ted began to notice how Lieutenant Shankster had become quite distressed and so he made the point of asking him if everything was satisfactory. To his amazement, the lieutenant answered by addressing him by his Christian name. Maybe, thought Ted, it was just a slip of the tongue, or then again it may well have been one of those friendly gestures between officer and servant which were so frowned upon by military traditionalists.

Ted was even more shocked when Lieutenant Shankster told him that on the previous night, he'd made out his will, as well as writing a long emotional letter to his parents in Grimsby, in which he truthfully expressed his real feelings toward them. He then handed both items to Ted, while at the same time requesting him to keep them in a safe place about his person, and should he not survive, then by fair means or foul, he wanted Ted to make sure they were despatched to his home address.

Trying everything possible to reassure the lieutenant that nothing whatsoever could cause any form of mishap, he could tell that his superior was completely oblivious to what was being said to him.

........................................

At the crack of dawn, the 17th Division consisting of 7th Lincolns, 10th Sherwoods, 8th Staffs and 7th Borders took Fricourt without any form of confrontation, Jerry having retreated to Fricourt Wood during the night. The actual village was a dreadful sight, being no more than an assemblage of ruins.

Advancing towards the wood was an experience which Ted would never be able to erase from his memory, for whichever way he looked there was war in all its brutal nakedness. Bodies were scattered in every direction, the end result of precision artillery fire.

Some poor devils were lying on their backs with eyes wide open, seemingly staring towards the heavens as if seeking absolution. Others, still clutching rifles were kneeling as if in prayer, while many without limbs, or in some instances without heads, were already providing sustenance for a large colony of marauding rats.

Equipment had been hurriedly abandoned by the German wounded, as losing all hope of survival and dignity, they were surrendering in great numbers. It mattered not to Tommy that these frightened young men coming towards them with hands raised high were the sworn enemy, for they like themselves were fellow mortals, with loved ones back home somewhere in Germany, who really did care about them.

From their far-off comfortable offices, it was the politicians who were responsible for starting wars, but unfortunately it was young enlisted soldiers who suffered the consequences.

The horrifying carnage on that day was indescribable, with most of the advancing infantrymen trying their utmost not to look, some even vomiting as their stomachs churned over at the appalling evilness of it all.

Upon reaching the three-quarter stage across the plain, German artillery erupted from well beyond the wood, many of their shells landing amongst the advancing 17th. So without warning it was now the British lads who were on the receiving end and included amongst the casualties were both officers and men with whom Ted had been well acquainted.

Just as those who were still in the land of the living began to think this could well be the start of their journey to kingdom come, British heavies again opened up with deadly accuracy, the outcome being that the division was able to continue its advance on Fricourt Wood.

Totally demoralised, enemy troops staggered out into the open with hands reaching for the sky and rifles and machine guns discarded. One particular officer came forward without his hands being raised, but when Lieutenant Shankster called to him to surrender, the man drew his revolver and shot the lieutenant through the forehead.

Throwing his weapon on the ground, the German then held both hands well above his head, as if to plead for mercy – but as Tommy so aptly put it – "some so-and-so chance he'd got."

This was the second officer Ted had lost and once again he felt it deeply. Always treating him more as a colleague than a subordinate, Lieutenant Shankster was as close to being the perfect gentleman as one could ever wish to meet. Unfortunately, sentimentality is of little comfort when taking part in armed conflict.

In battle, men react to certain situations in different ways. Some believe their paths can only lead to the day of judgement, while others reckon they are indestructible.

Lieutenant Shankster must have had some kind of premonition that he was about to die, otherwise it must be considered doubtful as to whether he would have made his will on the eve of battle. After all, he had been on infantry offensives previously.

The battalion entered a shell-violated Fricourt Wood during late afternoon, and less than one hour later, it was declared clear, but once again, at such a terrible price in human life.

Under cover of darkness, a battalion from the 51st Brigade arrived to take the place of the 7th Lincolns while they took a short forty-eight-hour reprieve from hell's kitchen, this being spent at Méaulte, just a few kilometres from the line.

**The Battle of the Somme, 1916**

# CHAPTER 16

## Satan's Garden

During the breathing space at Méaulte, Ted assembled his late officer's belongings and handed them over to the equipment sergeant, thereby abiding by military rules and regulations. Those particular items did not, however, include the lieutenant's last will and testament, for together with the letter written by Ted himself to Mr and Mrs Shankster, a separate delivery method had to be made.

Having received shrapnel wounds, Sergeant Alf Wiggins was being returned to Blighty to recuperate, and Ted, knowing of this, had purposely made his way to a nearby dressing station to see him. The outcome being that Alf agreed to post the package whenever convenient when he arrived in England.

...........................................

Back in the business of 'kill or be killed' the 7th Lincolns bypassed Fricourt village, before moving onto Pozières, which was situated on the Albert to Bapaume Road. Here they remained in reserve for two days, and then it was a night march towards Longueval, where they occupied a disused trench.

Having suffered heavy losses over a period of time, with insufficient replacements joining them, the entire 17th Division was temporarily relegated to the classification of 'relieving' division, as they were considered to be of insufficient strength to be able to make big all-out attacks on enemy positions.

During the first few nights, the lad's locations were heavily shelled, but as they'd spent the first day digging junk-holes in the trench sides, surprisingly few casualties were in evidence.

Just as Ted, Ted Paton and Jasper Houghton – three of the old 'Saddle-Room' gang – were holding a conversation in the trench bottom, a single shot from a sniper's rifle hit their machine-gunner in the head, causing him to fall across the parapet. Not knowing whether he was still alive, the three mates scrambled towards him, but just as Jasper raised his head a fraction higher than intended another shot rang out and he too fell dead.

ROLL OF HONOUR.—Few of the lads who are serving their King on land or sea could have been more respected or beloved by those who knew him than Jasper Houghton, the news of whose death was recently received by his parents. For them the greatest sympathy has been widely shown, not only in Colsterworth, but by many friends in the neighbourhood. Details of his death were not known till Saturday, when a letter from his friend and close companion, Pte. E. G. Dunkley, told how he volunteered to go out and bring back a wounded comrade. In this, it appears, he was successful, but, on reaching the trench he raised himself for a moment after the execution of his self-sacrificing effort, and was instantly killed by a sniper's bullet. His kindly and heroic action was entirely characteristic, and showed him to the last as thoughtful for others and as forgetful of self as he had always been.

A Colsterworth lad, Jasper had, on numerous occasions before the commencement of hostilities, played in sporting encounters against his two mates and later shared billets, barns and trenches with them, from Lincoln to The Somme. Now his lifeless body caused those same two pals considerable heartache. It was 10th July 1916 – yet another date that his two more fortunate colleagues would never forget.

Rolls of heavy gunfire gradually increased in volume to thunder-like magnitude, both in and around the large wooded area which lay ahead. The Lincolnshire lads were under strict orders to remain in their inadequate trench, until further notice, but Tommy being Tommy, he let everyone, irrespective of rank, know of his discontentment.

.........................................

After ten more days, which to Tommy seemed more like ten weeks, the order finally came through from HQ for the lads to move forward, together with the other battalions in the 17th to positions just outside Delville Wood. The terrifying sight ahead of them was not only one of complete devastation, with no vegetation whatsoever to protect them from enemy eyes, but the entire plain was strewn with hundreds of dead bodies, victims of ruthless artillery fire.

Eventually, an abandoned German trench was reached and orders filtered through for the division to use it as best they could as an overnight cover.

It became known that a few days earlier, the South African Brigade had moved in to take the wood, but as contact with them had been lost, it was assumed that something must have gone seriously wrong. In any case, the lads were informed it was far too risky to attempt further progress, at least until such time as the light improved.

Located in the central trench section, the Lincolns found themselves unable to grab forty winks, let alone several hours sleep, as the repulsive smell which wafted through the air from what was once a mass of mature trees simply wouldn't go away.

At the very first glimpse of the sun rising in the horizon's cleavage, stretcher-bearers were out and about, carrying out their usual brave but exhausting duties. Some of the missing South Africans were rescued, but whereas a few of them were able to relate dreadful details of how their colleagues were massacred by enemy artillery and machine-gun fire, they were unable to confirm how many, if indeed any others were still alive.

Shortly after six o'clock, orders were given for the division to enter Delville Wood – better known to Tommy as Devil's Wood – and to hold it at all costs.

Ted firmly believed that during his time on the Ypres Salient, he had experienced so much death and destruction it surely could not possibly get any worse. However, from that very moment he stepped foot into 'Devil's' he couldn't believe his own eyes, as lifeless, limbless and even decapitated blood-saturated bodies lay everywhere and in every position imaginable. The appalling nauseous stench was even worse than it had been the previous night.

Cautiously weaving their way around shell-distorted trees, with only their hideous charred stumps remaining, it was virtually impossible to make progress without falling over foul-smelling corpses. There was hardly a man who wasn't violently sick and almost all of them tied something or other across their mouths and noses in an attempt to prevent them from collapsing.

Amazingly, despite everything those heroic South Africans had been forced to endure, there were still a few of them who had made it through alive, but all the depleted 17th Division could offer them were drinks from their water bottles and to let them know that help was on the way.

As the sun's rays began to penetrate those ground-hugging smoke patches, the entire spectacle was far beyond the bounds of reality. Every single thing about the place symbolised spiritual darkness, almost as if it was the natural habitat of the damned, the awful stench adding the final touch to the devil's masterpiece. Could these young men from the shires of England's green and pleasant land be walking through Satan's garden?

Only later did it transpire that out of three and a half thousand men of the South African Brigade who entered 'Devil's Wood' on that fateful July morning, only some seven hundred and fifty escaped one week later. The majority of the survivors were severely disfigured and were unable to take any further part in the war.

Not only had those gallant men taken Delville Wood in the most murderous conditions imaginable, but their truly magnificent stand ranked alongside any in the annals of military history. What inconceivable hell they must have gone through. A relief from line duty is always welcome, but on this particular occasion it was an absolute godsend.

**The Devastation of Delville Wood**

Now only a shadow of its former strength, the division was withdrawn from The Somme, or at least it was until such time as more replacements arrived from the training camps in Blighty.

As the canvas billets, which the 7th Lincolns had been allocated at a ruined Fricourt, were now occupied by the 9th Northumberland Fusiliers, the 'Poachers' made a last-minute switch to Gommecourt, roughly midway between Albert and Arras. This gave the lads ample time to visit estaminets in or around the place during the evenings, enabling the slow inebriation from cheap wine to shut out those long nights of frightening nightmares about the horrors of Delville Wood.

.......................................

On the last day of July 1916, the 7th were informed of several changes being made in the chain of command. For some reason or other, the battalion's CO, Lieutenant Colonel Forrest, was relieved of his command and returned to England. His replacement was the newly promoted Major Metcalfe, CO of the 7th, but now promoted again to Lieutenant Colonel.

Lieutenant Colonel Metcalfe was highly respected by the men for he also wouldn't ask them to do anything which he wasn't prepared to do so himself.

A platoon of Tommies bypassing a ruined Fricourt village

Utter devastation – Fricourt Wood after the gunfire ceased.

# CHAPTER 17

## Zenith Trench

With little or nothing to keep the men active during daytime, many were given leave passes, some of the luckier ones making it to Blighty, but unfortunately Ted wasn't one of them.

When three weeks of inactivity turned to sheer boredom, the CO instructed his junior officers to innovate certain new assignments which hopefully would lift the spirits of those left in billets. The officers then enlisted the help of senior NCOs, and they too became involved in solving the problem.

Back from his enforced leave of absence in the South Lincolnshire countryside, Alf Wiggins newly promoted to Company Sergeant Major, approached quite a few of the lads, or at least the ones whom he regarded as being good mates, and asked them if they'd care to go on a leisurely machine-gun course at a really exquisite seaside resort. Most of them jumped at the idea, although one or two awkward ones, such as Ted, questioned whether it was absolutely necessary, simply because they'd previously been on a similar exercise at Wareham, yet still not one of them had fired a machine gun in anger.

.......................................

Under the command of Second Lieutenant Seaton, a recent addition to the Lincolns, a small unit of twenty men, made a 6am start from Gommecourt in a lorry which took them as far as Doullens. From there, it was a long train journey to Le Touquet before marching to the popular holiday resort of Paris-Plage, on the Channel coast.

The actual course really was an absolute picnic, finishing no later than 1pm daily, then it was off to the resort itself for a cooling-off period in the sea. A stroll along the promenade would follow, where tables and chairs were crammed full of middle-class French holidaymakers, all sitting beneath gaudy parasols, as if no war existed.

The colourful sails of distant yachts made a perfect background to this lovely scene, which was in complete contrast to what the lads in khaki were used to. War and all its horrors seemed a million miles away – and Ted for one hoped its blind fury would never ever be allowed to destroy such a tranquil location.

Without any doubt, the lads all agreed that Paris-Plage was the most pleasurable place in France that they had been to. All of them being young and single thoroughly enjoyed their ardent dalliances with the attractive mademoiselles, as well as paying visits to the town's estaminets and picture houses.

Pooling their remaining resources on the final day of the furlough, the lads purchased a bottle of the CSM's favourite tipple, for they were all very well aware that he must have pulled a few strings to wangle such a wonderful break from duties and all paid for courtesy of His Majesty's Army.

......................................

The happy party again returned to 'hell upon earth,' for the division's rest period had come to an end, and by the time the Paris-Plage contingent caught up with them, they were back in the line.

As October slipped into November, the 7th Borders were given the task of capturing the all-important Zenith trench, between Gueudecourt and Lesboeufs, which was known to be strongly fortified. Once taken, the 7th Lincolns – who were being held in reserve – were under orders to relieve them, then hold Zenith at all costs, for this really was the gateway to Bapaume, a town of great strategic importance to the enemy.

It was a pitch-black night when the Borders commenced their attack and many of their men became detached from the main assault group. Charging fast and furious, the Borders completely took Fritz by surprise, causing him to retreat rather rapidly.

Relieving the Borders, on the 3rd November, it soon transpired that the Germans still occupied part of the same trench. Speedily informing HQ of the unprecedented situation, instructions were requested. A plan of action was hastily formulated and was scheduled to be put into operation within thirty minutes.

Bombing officers and their subordinates arrived and several 7th Lincolnshire lads, Ted included, were detailed to fix bayonets and accompany them. They were told that it was essential for the attack to be carried out without artillery assistance, owing to the close proximity of the two warring factions.

Taken unexpectedly from the rear, every single German was either killed or captured.

Captain Pennington of 'A' Company, who planned the attack, was awarded the DSO while Second Lieutenant Williams, the bombing officer, received the MC. Captain Lindley and 2nd Lieutenant Thomas were also awarded the MC, and Private Richer was awarded the DCM.

Unfortunately, the 'PBI', who'd carried out the lion's share of the operation, gained no form of recognition whatsoever, but as Tommy remarked later – "What's new?"

On that third evening, 'B' Company lost another officer, when Lieutenant Seaton reported 'sick' with trench foot and dysentery. He was returned to England, where he became a patient in a hospital at Mansfield, after which, as far as anyone was aware, he never returned to France.

..........................................

It was sometime during the morning of Lieutenant Seaton's departure that Ted experienced one of the narrowest escapes imaginable. To him, his deliverance from eternal rest was about as close to a miracle as anyone could possibly get, though regrettably the same incident proved fatal for a highly esteemed colleague.

Together with Sergeant Charlie Cooper and Ernie Warner, two old members of the 'Saddle-Room' gang Ted stood side by side in their shallow trench, while Captain Barnes, OC 'B' Company, was map-reading close by. In order to obtain a closer view of the officer, Charlie moved Ted slightly to one side, before leaning over and saying, "Excuse me sir, but is that Le Transloy over there?"

Before the captain was able to reply, a sniper's bullet struck Charlie in the head causing him to fall backwards into the trench bottom.

Whether or not the marksman's deadly missile was intended for Ted would never be known, but there was little doubt that if Charlie hadn't moved him when he did, the outcome may very well have been different.

Sergeant John Charles Cooper MM really was a splendid individual. Acting as CSM he was one of life's gentlemen. A married man with two young children back in England, he would be genuinely missed by everyone in the battalion who knew him.

That night Ted and Ernie buried Charlie in his temporary resting place, placing a rough wooden cross close to where his head lay. The trio had been good mates since early training days, and his three stripes made no difference whatsoever to that friendship.

The awesome Thiepval Memorial where vast numbers of British and Commonwealth troops are commemorated in perpetuity by the Commonwealth War Grave Commission.

The large amount of names include Sgt John Charles Cooper (M.M.) and 2nd Lt Stanley Shankster (see pages 103 and 116).

# CHAPTER 18

## Christmas in Hospital

Extended stints in the line, similar to those experienced on the Ypres Salient, were gradually being reduced. Sir Douglas Haig's new policy of only allowing his troops in trenches for shorter spells was much appreciated by officers and men alike.

"Men are not machines you know," Haig was reported as saying, and Tommy couldn't agree more. What a pity those self-centred old buffers at GHQ didn't think likewise when they were dictating their abysmal trench warfare strategy, earlier in the conflict. Fortunately for front-line Tommy, Sir Douglas realised just how incompetent they were, and he began to arrange for some of them to be retired or given desk jobs back in Blighty. Even so, quite a number managed to slip the net and remain in their pretentious positions.

Eventually, the time arrived for the 17th Division's withdrawal from the Somme. No departing for a long period of intensive training, nor yet a move to a quieter part of the front this time – instead it was to be a complete removal from 'hell and all its fury', to recharge its power source. Moving well clear of the line, they marched back to Méaulte, just below Albert.

Settling down for the day, Ted was approached by an orderly, who asked him to report to Lieutenant Squires immediately. This particular officer had already acknowledged him on two previous occasions during his forty-eight hour break from line duty, as the two of them knew each other from the time Ted was batman to Lieutenant Hayward.

Originally coming out to France with the 7th Lincolns when their training programme at Bovington Camp was concluded, he was soon sent back to England to recuperate, following an illness. Now fully fit again, he had been given the all-clear to resume normal combat duties.

Entering a makeshift office, Ted was quite startled to be greeted with a firm handshake and asked to take a seat.

"First of all, I'd like to say how sorry I was to learn of Charlie Hayward's death. I know how well you and he got on, as he always spoke highly of you."

Muttering some seemingly inadequate reply before the lieutenant went on to say, "Now I'll come straight to the point, for you see I'm in urgent need of a servant and I firmly believe you would fit the bill admirably. So, I wonder if it is possible for me to persuade you to accept the position?"

Anticipating this may well be the question Lieutenant Squires would put to him, Ted asked for time to consider the matter, for he made it clear that he'd already lost two fine officers after a short period of time, and he had no desire to be put through the same anguish again.

The following morning, Ted again knocked on the officer's door and accepted the offer. The two of them shook hands and sealed the agreement over a glass of the finest scotch.

Remembering that Lieutenant Hayward had once told him that Lieutenant Squires was the most unorthodox officer in the British Army, Ted couldn't help but wonder just what he'd let himself in for.

Having packed their belongings, the 7th, marched off to Dernancourt railhead, where they boarded first-class cattle trucks to travel to a small town named Picquigny, just a few kilometres north-west of Amiens.

Arriving ahead of the battalion, the officers found themselves reasonable billets, with Lieutenant Squires managing to get himself fixed up in a fine-looking house in the town centre. He'd also negotiated with the owners for Ted to have a room on the ground floor. What a lovely old couple the householders were, refusing point blank to allow Ted to carry out any kind of domestic chores whatsoever. They insisted on providing the two Englishmen's meals, making endless jugs of coffee and even washing and ironing their dirty laundry. In fact, they even insisted upon making their beds as well.

Both man and wife were really genuinely delightful and Ted's only regret was that their command of the English language wasn't any better than his French. Nevertheless, they had great fun trying to converse with each other.

Lieutenant Squires was such an easy-going officer where Ted was concerned, that his working day began at 8am, and finished at 9am, then it was off with the lads to discover the delights of Picquigny.

After being in the town for only two weeks, the lieutenant received orders to pack up and return to Méaulte, where he was to undergo a Stokes Trench Mortar training course, and quite naturally Ted was expected to accompany him. Neither of them was any too pleased about the sudden change in plan, as both were enjoying the kind of life they were leading, the mutual goodwill between townspeople and Tommy being *par excellence*.

With Lieutenant Squires' time being taken up on the course all day, Ted had precious little to do, other than play cards with other officers' servants. However, at the end of ten days the training programme came to its conclusion and officer and batman packed their bags and returned to their billets in Picquigny. The elderly couple at the house were as pleased to see them again as they were to see their hosts.

After enjoying three more days relaxing with their respective colleagues, the Lieutenant was again the recipient of yet another order, this time instructing him to make his way to a village by the name of Vaux-en-Amienois, where he was to attend an advanced seven-day trench mortar course. To say that he was a shade unhappy about it was an understatement, as he repeatedly cursed everyone from the CO right up to Haig, for ruining his highly enjoyable rest period.

.......................................

As before, it was a case of officers being fully occupied with course work, while their batmen thumb-twiddled.

Noticing that Ted was decidedly disillusioned with his situation, Lieutenant Squires suggested he borrow a bicycle and take a ride over to HQ at Picquigny, to see if there was any mail for the two of them.

Next morning, the 9th December, Ted was joined by two fellow batmen whose officers were friends of Lieutenant Squires, one being with the 8th South Staffs and the other with the 7th Borders.

It was not often that Tommy had the good fortune to go cycle riding through the picturesque French countryside, but the trio rode off with great enthusiasm. Letters and parcels were collected from the Lincolns' HQ, then it was on to Soues to do the same at the Borders' HQ before completing their task at Reincourt, where the Staffs were resting. A good meal was provided here, after which it was back to Vaux-en-Amienois via

Cavillon, Fourdrinoy, Breilly, Ailly-sur-Somme and St Sauveur.

Upon arrival at the billets, they were greeted with the dreadful news of an accident which had occurred at the mortar range during firing practice, and that several officers were either killed or severely wounded. The scene, it seems, resembled that of a battlefield dressing station, with limbs being gathered together and ambulances rushing off at breakneck speed in an attempt to get the injured to hospital at Amiens.

The 7th Borders' officer, whose batman rode with the other two to collect mail, was one of those killed, while the South Staffs' officer and Lieutenant Squires were both seriously injured.

Instructed to gather all of his officer's possessions, and put them on a limber to be taken to the No 1 New Zealand Stationary Hospital at Amiens, Ted found five other batmen doing likewise. Upon arrival, the personal effects were taken care of by hospital staff and each batman was told that a large room had been made available for them, until further notice. This meant that Ted and his new mates had nothing to do all day, other than to visit estaminets and coffee shops.

Never had any of them thought it at all possible that such a marvellous life could exist in the British Army, especially as an all-out war was raging not too far distant. Through no fault of their own, the six lads were having the time of their lives while front-line troops desperately needed replacements for those who'd been killed or wounded.

The festive season arrived and what a splendid time they all had. New Zealand staff all received huge amounts of food parcels from home and on Christmas Day they put on a banquet fit for a king.

During the two weeks in which Lieutenant Squires had been in hospital, Ted had only been allowed to see him on three occasions, and even then he was permitted to stay no longer than five minutes at any one time.

Early in 1917, Lieutenant Squires was returned to Blighty, and such were his wounds that Ted did not expect to see him again.

Returning to the 7th Lincolns new HQ at Ginchy, some ten kilometres south of Bapaume, Ted resumed the duties of an infantryman.

# CHAPTER 19

# Exuberance and Despondency

During the middle of January 1917, the 17th Division returned to the Somme, this time taking over trenches on the Combles Section, slightly west of Sailly-Salllise.

Severe frosts lasted throughout the month and almost up to the end of February, making everywhere so bitterly cold. Water-filled shell-holes were frozen solid as was the usual sea of mud, thus making life almost unbearable. Weeks of thick fog lay across the entire region, thereby adding a certain degree of eeriness to Tommy's plight.

Suffering dreadfully with frostbite, many men were taken out of the line and sent for hospital treatment, leaving the action zone woefully weak. But of course if Tommy was feeling disadvantaged, so too was Fritz.

Under such daunting conditions, it was obvious that neither side wished to become involved in serious rabble-rousing and quite frankly who could blame them.

During all those weeks of severe atmospheric conditions, officers were rarely seen, choosing instead to remain in their warm Saps. Good old-fashioned English breakfasts were served to them in bed and for lunch it was steak and dried vegetables, with a can of fruit for dessert, followed by cheese and biscuits with a glass or two of the best French wine. Meanwhile, trench Tommy had to make do with his frozen bully and rock-hard biscuits. No wonder the front-line soldier reckoned there was no justice in the British Army.

The 7th Lincolns had been in and out of the line for longer periods than of late, with rest intervals lasting only three or four days. So much for Haig's bright idea of infantrymen only spending short stints at the front at any one time. How his name was cursed by every man who had to tolerate the wretched icy, cold conditions with inadequate rations and insufficient clothing to prevent them from freezing to death.

Young lads, many of whom had been in the service for less than six months, were often in tears and it was left to the old hands to give them whatever encouragement they could.

At long last the great thaw began and overnight everything turned into a rich chocolate-brown pudding-mix swamp. Trenches and dugouts were knee-deep in the stuff and it even gushed into the officers' Saps. Poets and songwriters may have described it as 'mud, mud glorious mud', but that was not how Tommy referred to it, as his no-frills decription was a shade more unrefined.

..........................................

At last, the 17th was withdrawn from the Combles Sector, but for some unknown reason, the 7th Lincolns rest period was spent on what seemed like a marching tour of the French countryside, north-west of Amiens.

Sometimes, the lads were allocated half-reasonable huts in which to spend the nights, though more often than not, it turned out to be the proverbial bed of straw in some remote barn. Once again, the weather turned bitterly cold and to make matters even worse, little or no provision had been made available for cooking or heating. Little wonder that Tommy was forced to turn to crime to ensure his survival.

The battalion having been split into smaller groups of one hundred or so men, made it easier to organise.

Raiding parties were divided into separate units, with one of them 'borrowing' wooden fencing, railway sleepers or the occasional wooden hut, in order that fires could be made, while others pilfered food supplies, mainly from army-storage buildings, which the lads had made a mental note of en route. Naturally, what they were doing was illegal, but as Tommy said, "better that than freeze to death."

Wherever the men's overnight billet happened to be, so the very same ritual occurred, causing annoyance amongst the local population. Villagers complained to officers, who in turn complained to the NCOs and they, who were enjoying the fruits of the lads' labours, casually mentioned it to Tommy. But Tommy being Tommy took not the slightest bit of notice.

Arriving at a village by the name of Rougefay, north-east of Auxi-le-Chateau, the lads were surprised to find themselves being ushered into a large building, similar in design to a village institute back home in Blighty. Inside they found trestle tables, wooden benches, piles of blankets and a good old-fashioned log fire roaring away in an iron stove. Hurricane lamps had been lit and placed on shelving along each wall and both the tricolour and the Union Jack hung side by side at the rear of a small stage.

A well-spoken elderly gentleman appeared and made a short speech in excellent English, before asking everyone present to make themselves comfortable, while the ladies of Rougefay served them with tea and home-made biscuits. And how well made and appetising they were too!

Unknown to the Lincolnshire lads, the inhabitants had on the previous day been informed of their impending arrival, the outcome being that a village meeting was hastily called and they all agreed to pool resources in an all-out effort to provide each khaki-clad guest with a hearty meal. And what a splendid meal it turned out to be.

It seems the well-spoken gentleman was quite a wealthy land owner and he'd made arrangements for some of his employees to remove the carcass of one of his oxen from a cold store and cut it up for the ladies to cook especially for the occasion. All the villagers provided vegetables, and when those lovely madames and mademoiselles entered the room, each carrying steaming hot meals for the lads to eat, without any hesitation whatsoever, they all stood up and applauded. Dumbfounded, they devoured the feast like a pack of hungry wolves.

Afterwards, there was an excellent choice of quality cakes, as well as cheese and biscuits. When these were finished off, the men folk brought in a barrel of their very own make of brandy.

One of the better educated lads stood up and, in a mixture of French and English, thanked their hosts for providing such magnificent hospitality. There was certainly no doubting that the exceptional generosity and warmth of welcome given by those genuinely friendly people did more to promote entente-cordiale than anything the lads had experienced since first disembarking from the boat at Boulogne.

......................................

Within a few days the entire 7th Battalion gathered together and marched into Doullens, where they were scheduled to rendezvous with the 8th Sherwoods and 8th South Staffs, before moving yet again to the dreaded Somme.

In view of the remarkable military build-up in Doullens, the whole town was chock-a-block. Told by the CSM that they could stretch their legs if they so wished but to be back within the hour, the lads hurriedly dispersed. Ambling along the main shopping area, Ted watched another large convoy of lorries, each towing heavy guns, come to a halt and he remembered thinking to himself that something really big must be in the air.

Gazing into shop windows, Ted suddenly heard his name being called, and upon looking around, he was stunned to see two of his brothers jumping off one of the lorries and running towards him. What a huge shock it was, and what an unbelievable stroke of luck, Ted being every bit as delighted to see them as Arthur and Frank were to see him.

Shaking hands and hugging each other, they were completely oblivious of others watching. Chin-wagging for well nigh on thirty minutes, they exchanged news snippets from home and it was only when the convoy began to move again, that the happy trio had to say their goodbyes – just to think, of the five brothers serving with the B.E.F., three of them had met up by pure chance. What a story to write and tell the folks back home.

......................................

March the 23rd 1917 was indeed a day that Ted would never ever forget, for that was the very last time he saw his brother Frank alive.

Just a few days later – March 31st to be exact – Frank was standing on guard duty outside his overnight billet, a mere two kilometres behind the front line, slightly north of Arras, when an enemy shell exploded very close by. Severely injured by the blast and iron fragments, brother Arthur helped to carry him to a dressing station, but tragically he died the following day.

Within one week, Ted had gone from a feeling of exuberance to one of despondency.

Continually thinking of his parents back home in Market Harborough and of how heartbroken they would be, he also felt for Arthur and of the terrible anguish which he too must be feeling. Both he and Frank had enlisted together at the outbreak of hostilities and were serving in the 60th Siege Battery, Royal Garrison Artillery.

The very thing which upset Ted most of all, was the fact that he couldn't be at home with his mother and father, at a time when they desperately needed the family around them.

And, of course, he knew that Arthur would be feeling exactly the same. Naturally, he had written to his parents immediately upon hearing the awful news, but under the circumstances, a mere letter seemed totally inadequate.

| Arthur | Ted | Frank |

**Three Brothers —**
**taken in Doullens; a week later Frank was killed**

# CHAPTER 20

# Blessing in Disguise

When the Battle of Arras commenced on the 9th April 1917, the 17th Division was being kept in reserve at Berneville, an average-sized village, five kilometres or so, south-west of the city.

Strolling along the main thoroughfare in Berneville with five mates, Ted unexpectedly bumped into his former officer, Lieutenant Squires, but by now he had beenpromoted to captain. It seems that he'd quite recently returned to active service, after recuperating from the injuries he'd received in the mortar-shell accident.

Captain Squires returned the small group's smart salutes before holding out a hand towards Ted, and the pair of them shook hands as enthusiastically as if two old friends encountering each other after several years of being apart.

Informing Ted that officially he was still with the 7th Lincolns, he had nevertheless been upgraded to the rank of captain in order to become OC of the newly formed 51st Trench Mortar Battery. In effect, this was a support unit of the 17th Division. He then went on to say, that at the present time he was busy recruiting reliable men from the division to join the new venture.

Changing the subject completely, he also said that he'd found it necessary to fix himself up with another batman as upon making enquiries about Ted's whereabouts, a colleague had informed him that he thought he'd been wounded or possibly killed.

"Anyhow, not to worry about it old chap, I'm glad to know you're still very much with us."

Pausing for a few moments, the captain went on to say, "Now then, I've got just the job for you."

Looking somewhat puzzled, Ted replied, "And exactly what would that be sir?"

"Well this is hardly the place to discuss it, but if you'd pop into my billet during the afternoon, I'll be glad to put you in the picture."

Ted saluted and replied, "Yes sir." The two of them shook hands again and Captain Squires strode off to a nearby French officer's army hut.

Once out of sight, Ted's mates returned, after making themselves scarce, and immediately began to pull his leg about fraternising with the enemy.

Charlie Wright said, "I've seen every bloody thing now, but a captain shaking hands with a bloody private must surely be the be-all and end-all."

"You can tell exactly what's going to happen," laughed Charlie Boon. "By this time tomorrow, he'll have been made-up to a bloody CSM, and then he'll be telling us all what we can and can't do."

Taking all the humorous banter in good spirit, Ted explained that the captain was known to be a bit of a loose cannon and that military correctness was not always at the top of his list of priorities.

Midway through the afternoon, Ted knocked on the captain's billet door and immediately he called, "come in, come in," followed by "pull up a seat, there's a good chap."

Ted did as he was told and waited for the officer to continue.

"Now, as I've already mentioned, I am taking over the 51st TMB and therefore I'm in urgent need of adaptable and trustworthy men to ensure that the whole venture works effectively. As I know you pretty well, I'd like you to take over one of the batteries. This will mean your immediate promotion to sergeant, of course, then within a month, you'd be made-up to CSM, which considering your age and frontline experience is no less than you should be. Now then, are you prepared to do that?"

Momentarily, Ted was absolutely dumbfounded, for what he was being offered was totally unexpected. However, pulling himself together, he answered, "Well thank you sir. Yes I would very much like to join your new set-up, but there's no way I wish to accept any form of promotion."

Trying his utmost to get his former batman to change his mind, Captain Squires finally gave up, as he was well aware that Ted possessed a stubborn streak, therefore realising it would be pointless in pursuing the matter.

"Well, I'd still be glad to have you with us, and stripes or no stripes, you would be put in charge of one of the batteries, and if at all possible try your best to get your five mates to come along with you."

Later the same evening, Ted and his pals discussed the possibility of joining-up with the TMBs and after considerable debate, all five put their names forward.

Following the completion of the necessary paperwork, they went along with about thirty other lads from the 17th for extensive training on Stokes Mortar guns.

Heavy fighting was taking place along the Feuchy line which was on the Arras-Douai railway, five kilometres east of Arras. First reports coming in indicated considerable gains were being made along a fairly broad front, with cavalry breaking enemy lines in several places. Unfortunately, the following day, further dispatches confirmed a retreat was in progress. It seems that glue-pot conditions, barbed-wire and the deadly accuracy of Fritz's machine gunners were responsible for both men and horses being mown down, leaving very many killed or seriously wounded.

Several days elapsed, after which a request was made for the 51st TMBs to assist the 51st Brigade, as several of their own batteries had been wiped out by heavy shell fire.

Entering Arras from Dainville it was apparent that the suburbs had received very little attention from enemy artillery, though upon reaching the city centre, especially the square, buildings lay in ruins, very much reminiscent of Ypres.

An overnight stop was made at St Nicholas camp, then early next morning a somewhat circuitous route was taken to Blangy. Just a few weeks earlier, both places were in German hands, but the sheer determination of the infantry battalions had forced Fritz to withdraw or surrender.

In Feuchy, the TMBs were made to take evasive action beneath a steep woodland bank, due to severe shelling. Eventually, this came to an abrupt halt and the batteries were moved alongside a narrow-gauge railway track by the River Scarpe.

Splitting them into individual units, Captain Squires then made an advanced reconnaissance in order to select appropriate gun positions, thereby leaving Lieutenants Tyrrel, Ramsden and Hoyton in charge.

While waiting for the OC to return, Jerry again opened with heavy shellfire and once again the lads were compelled to take refuge. Ted and his crew of five immediately jumped into the nearest shell crater, praying to whoever their God might be that lightning wouldn't strike in the same place twice. But as soon as the barrage ended and they were able to scramble out of their temporary sanctuary, they were shocked to find that four members of another gun crew had been killed and two more seriously injured. And to cap it all, both mortar guns were damaged beyond repair.

Having escaped the onslaught, Lieutenant Tyrell instructed the six survivors to return along the Scarpe in an effort to trace the other four batteries. However, amongst all the wild horror and confusion, this was virtually impossible, although they did manage to make contact with the 7th Lincolns, who had been brought into the action, after trench holding duties between Feuchy and Lone Copse. It seems their immediate objective was to capture the village of Pelves, close to the Scarpe.

Meanwhile, the rest of the battalion was attacking along the right-hand bank of the river, while the 5th Division was doing likewise alongside the left bank.

Explaining the crew's predicament to one of the 7th officers, Ted asked what they should do under the circumstances, and it was suggested to him that the best solution would be to remain with the division then try to resolve the matter later. The lads readily agreed, so for the time being they were back in the old routine as infantrymen.

......................................

At the first shimmer of a new dawn, a tremendous noise erupted as British Artillery bombarded Jerry's lines close to Bayonet and Rifle Trenches.

Gun flashes leapt out from cunningly concealed places and all hell was let loose. Each man, including the six TMB lads, waiting apprehensively to go over the top, must have thought judgement day had arrived, for the sheer professionalism of those gunners was absolutely awesome. It was as Arthur Perrins so aptly put it, "Thank God they're on our side and not Fritz's."

As the barrage lifted, so the infantry went about their ruthless business, many of them for the very first and last, time.

Crazed with fear, some of them raced forward, shouting obscenities in an attempt to relieve intense pressure, while others were impaled on isolated pieces of barbed-wire spikes. For a short time, German machine gunners had a field day cutting the lads down with the ease of highly polished experts.

It wasn't all one-sided though, as a great many attackers stormed the German line like men driven by demons.

All day long the battle raged, until Fritz dropped back nearer to the Hindenberg Line. Ground had been gained by the sheer tenacity and commitment of those incredible foot soldiers, but at such a high cost in human life.

Numbers of hitherto happy-go-lucky young men would never again hear the beautiful sound of a dawn chorus, or see an awe-inspiring sunset over distant horizons.

In life, every front-line soldier is dominated by power and rank, but death is such a great equaliser; it doesn't recognise status.

On this particular occasion, the 7th Lincolns fared better than most of the 17th Division, coming through some of the worst fighting almost unscathed, and they were able to help the stretcher-bearers bring back the badly injured, while the walking wounded hobbled along as best they could.

Having received so many losses, the entire 17th was taken out of the line – God only knew, it certainly needed time to rehabilitate itself.

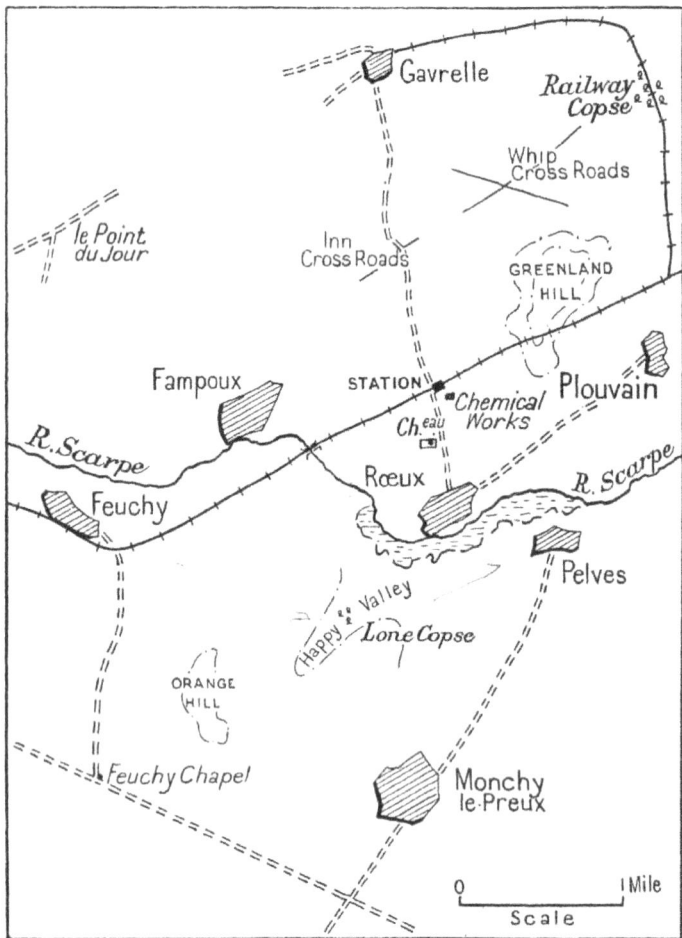

THIRD BATTLE OF THE SCARPE, 1917

# CHAPTER 21

## Down on the Farm

Having tried desperately to locate the whereabouts of absent members of the 51st TMB, Ted again found it necessary to speak with one of the 7th's officers, in the hope of coming up with some kind of agreement over his teams short-term future. Once more, however, he was instructed to remain with the Lincolns until such time that he received fresh orders.

Together with the battalion's 'B' Company boys the TMB lads were despatched to Beaudricourt, a village ten kilometres north east of Doullens, for the rest period they so desperately needed. Once in the village, they occupied conventional farm buildings with the accustomed beds of straw.

Anything in dairy produce, such as milk, chickens, beef, eggs etc could be purchased from the farmer's wife, for a modest fee, thus enabling the cooks to develop their culinary skills with a little more flair than usual.

By the time a fortnight had elapsed, the lads were becoming seriously short of funds, for they hadn't been paid in over a month. But Tommy being Tommy, he complained bitterly to the NCOs, who in turn mentioned the rumblings of discontent to the officers, but all they could do was offer sympathy as they too were in the same unfortunate position.

Every man in the 7th was fully aware that money needed to be raised. Serious situations called for serious action, thus causing many of the lads to sell anything they could lay their hands on, whether by fair means or foul.

One Tommy sold a pair of officer's binoculars to the landlord of one of the estaminets. Another stole a rifle and sold it to the farmer's wife, while yet another broke into the officers' mess and stole a couple of bottles of Scotch and then sold them to a prominent member of the gendarmerie.

One enterprising lad from Louth 'borrowed' a saw, an axe and a heavy long-handled sledgehammer from a visiting Royal Engineers' lorry and he also sold them to the farmer's wife. It wasn't that he intended taking them, but as he said later on, somehow or other, they just seemed to fall into his hands when passing.

Everyone was aware of the rumour that the farmer's wife would purchase anything that was on offer, providing the price was right, as it seems she ran a nice little earner on the side, buying and selling whatever was available. Tommy, of course knew of this, so when she paid out cash for any item stolen, both parties were happy.

The unfortunate thing about the tools stolen from the Engineers was that as soon as they discovered they were missing, they brought in the military police. When questioned each and every one of the lads put on a deliberate act of indignation. Meanwhile, knowing that the farmer's wife was away from the house, the offender nipped through the rear door with the intention of 'borrowing' them back again.

Unable to trace any of the items on the ground floor, he raced upstairs where, upon opening the very first bedroom door that he came to, he could hardly believe his own eyes, for there right in front of him was an Aladdin's cave of extremely dodgy merchandise – rifles, ammunition, khaki clothing, officers' coats, groundsheets, tin helmets, blankets, boots, tins of food, pots of jam, whisky, rum, tools galore – in fact, almost anything short of a howitzer.

Recovering the three tools, the Louth lawbreaker cunningly restored them to their rightful owner, in the hope that when one of the MPs or Engineers returned to the lorry, they would come across them – and this is exactly what happened.

Apologising with considerable embarrassment, the Engineers and MPs were sent packing with words of stinging admonishment ringing in their ears. Even the lad from Louth, who was responsible for the mayhem couldn't resist adding insult to injury.

Amongst the many items the resourceful Tommy had noticed in the farmer's back bedroom were several crates of good quality wine, and when mentioning this to his circle of mates, they immediately thought it would be a good idea to 'borrow' a few bottles. So while two of them kept a lookout on the movements of the farmer and his wife, the Louth petty pilferer and two accomplices were able to sneak into the house undetected and remove 'one or two bottles' – or to be more precise, a crate apiece!

That evening 'B' Company, which was reduced to less than eighty men, plus the six TMB lads, drank the whole lot. Afterwards they filled the empty bottles with water, and the next day returned them from whence they came.

If anyone was to blame for such incidents cropping up, it was indeed, the powers that be in the pay offices of the British Army, for making Tommy wait far too long, for what was rightfully his. As the rest period progressed, so 'B' Company gradually turned into highly skilled criminals in order to survive.

Working in agriculture before enlistment, several Tommies really did delight in helping out on the farm, for not only were the farmer and his wife a charming couple, but the actual feeling of them being close to the land again was a huge boost to their peace of mind. Also, it was apparent that none of them relished the idea of the time when they'd have to return to being front-line soldiers again.

On the very last evening of their rest period, the farmer and his wife organised a farewell feast for all the lads. A barn had been cleaned and decorated for the occasion, and yet again, what a marvellous meal they served up. Whether or not this was a French tradition, the whole event was a repetition of the last night spent at Rougefay.

Not only was the food splendidly cooked and presented in expert fashion by the ladies of the village, but also the wine flowed freely, that is unless you happened to be one of the unlucky ones who received a bottle which Tommy had replaced with water!

Finally, the moment arrived when the lads had to say au-revoir to Beaudricourt, for there was still a war to be won and the 7th Lincolns were needed to play their part.

# CHAPTER 22

# Blighty

During the whole of May 1917 the 7th Lincolns were in and out of trenches between Fampoux and Gavrelle, north of the Scarpe. Between times, very short periods of respite were spent at the infamous St Nicholas Camp.

Occasionally, both sides in the conflict would become quite cantankerous towards one another, more often than not, resulting in ferocious outbursts of artillery fire. Confusion and chaos reigned in each other's back yards, thereby causing many more good men to meet their maker much sooner than they had anticipated.

One of the big stumbling blocks which prevented ground troops from making progress was the massive chemical factory near to Fampoux. In fact, it had been taken and lost so many times both Fritz and Tommy were in the habit of leaving notes for each other.

Using the building as an observation post, it gave Jerry clear unobstructed views of the British lines, although Tommy couldn't help but notice that all high buildings in enemy-held territory were left untouched by British guns, and this was always an irascible bone of contention. Orders from GHQ to respect French property hampered the artillery boys throughout the entire war, often causing bitter disappointment and frustration. To the gunners, it really was a sore point, especially as Fritz had no such scruples.

For the very same reason, Vitry-en-Artois clock tower was left completely unblemished, yet every division which fought along the Scarpe knew to their cost that it too was being used as a vantage point. It really was the perfect example of Tommy's life being less important than bricks and mortar. Most certainly, the lads at the front who stood to suffer most on account of such a crackbrained policy began to wonder if our own generals had defected to the other side.

Eventually, the chemical works was recaptured by the 4th Division, and again Fritz left his little annotations telling Tommy to leave the place in a reasonable condition as he'd soon be back. Tommy's response was typical but preferably not to be read by the ladies' knitting circle!

..........................................

During the early hours of the third Friday in the month, there was a violent thunderstorm, which erupted sporadically throughout the day. It was certainly the worst the lads had experienced since stepping onto French soil, and in next to no time, dugouts and trenches were awash with squelching porridge-like mud. Soaked to the skin, the lads at least had the consolation of knowing whatever problems they were experiencing, so too was Fritz.

Sometime around midday, rifle fire began to emanate from the German trenches, some eight hundred metres distant. Immediately, everyone in the British line took rapid precautionary action, but as no one saw or heard any tell-tale signs, such as bullets hitting ramparts or what was left of the tree stumps, it very quickly became apparent to Tommy that there must be another reason for the sudden disruption.

Pulling himself to the top of the trench, the CSM was able to get a better view of what was happening with the aid of field glasses. Almost immediately, he began to chortle, and then within a few seconds, the chortling became thigh-slapping laughter. Soon afterwards he slid back to the hurriedly made ledge on the side of the trench, where the lads were eagerly awaiting some sort of explanation.

"You'd not believe this in a month o' Sundays," laughed the CSM, "but believe it or not, Fritz is actually shooting rats, bloody rats of all things."

At that precise moment, a rather repulsive looking long-tailed rodent surfaced from the brown mire below and attempted to make its escape over the parapet, but with a short sharp pull on the trigger, Charlie Wright sent it on its way to the next world.

"Tek that you bloody mangy sod," yelled Charlie, "And don't bloody well come back either."

"It'd have a bit of a job," quipped the CSM, "considering you just about took its bleedin' head off from a range of six feet."

For the next ten minutes 'B' Company exercised their own shooting skills, with the large rat colony making good target practice.

While the high-spirited vermin shoot was taking place, the CSM took a further look at Fritz's line, and the very first thing that caught his eye was a German officer doing exactly the same, but naturally in the opposite direction. Recognising the English lads were doing the same as his own, he waved in an understanding manner – the CSM doing likewise.

If only war was that simple…

...........................................

On the last day of the month, the 17th Division was relieved by the 34th. This meant the Poachers were destined for another rest period, this time in a village named Pommera, which they were told was near to Doullens.

Tommy did what he always did. He marched the thirty kilometres to Pommera, and this was after spending long periods in the line with just a few short rest intervals.

Arriving in the place, wet, cold and footsore, the 7th were as usual, accommodated in barns with straw spread out over the floor. Officers had taken furnished rooms in the farmhouse while NCOs occupied a recently erected army hut close by.

........................................

Having been in Pommera for a couple of days, Ted bumped into Lieutenant Tyrrell from the 51st TMBs, who told him that the first mission had been a total disaster. Amongst all the chaos that had taken place, each individual mortar-gun crew had gone missing and that Captain Squires had temporarily abandoned the entire set-up until such time it could be reviewed. He also went on to say that the Captain was on leave in Blighty and that no decision would be made until after his return.

Discussing the unfairness of the 'leave' system that same evening, Ted and Charlie Wright decided to approach Lieutenant Tyrell the following morning to see if there was any possibility of them both securing Blighty tickets as they considered them to be well overdue.

Listening intently to the argument put forward, the Lieutenant promised to take the matter up when he visited the Lincolns HQ the next day. The outcome was successful and produced two leave passes for 14 days apiece. To say they were ecstatic was putting it rather mildly.

The ruling regarding men proceeding on leave to England was simple and straightforward. Each man was supposed to be issued with a complete new uniform, including underclothing and boots, but trying to convince a quartermaster sergeant that such a regulation existed was akin to asking a bull terrier to sit when a cat crosses its path.

Always appearing to be miserable souls, they distributed new uniforms almost as if they'd paid for them out of their own pockets. Not that they denied themselves the very best of military attire mind you, for no one in the entire British Army ever saw a QMS looking tatty.

Having finally persuaded the pompous NCO that replacement uniforms were an absolute necessity, he reluctantly agreed to issue them. Regimental flashes were hurriedly sewn on, and afterwards, Lieutenant Ramsden gave them fourteen-day warrants and one hundred and fifty francs apiece and wished them bon voyage.

With no transport readily available, the duo walked to Mondicourt railhead, and from there it was a long slow journey to Abbeville. Here they slept on hard, wooden benches beneath the stars, as it was impossible to get overnight accommodation.

Early next morning, it was on to Boulogne, and then onto the leave boat to Folkestone. Almost before realising it, the train was speeding along through the lovely Kent countryside and on to St Pancras.

Alighting onto the platform at Market Harborough station, there was an unexpected welcoming party, for there stood sister Eadie and brothers Arthur and Harry, who were both home on leave from France. The last time Ted had seen Arthur, was in the main street of Doullens, just a few days before Frank was killed.

There's certainly no place quite like home and only those who've experienced face-to-face confrontation with the Angel of Death can begin to understand such deep-seated emotion.

Ted's parents had visually aged since he last saw them and it was more than obvious that they were still devastated by Frank's death, even though they both tried to hide the fact.

Early next morning, Harry had to return to his unit, so Ted and Arthur walked with him to the railway station.

What a wonderful feeling it was to be able to sit in the front room at 71 Caxton Street, talking about the nicer things in life, almost as if war was just a figment of the imagination. Ted and Arthur purposely making no mention of the many times they'd often wondered if the very next bullet or shell would have their name on it.

The two brothers were delighted to be sharing a room, more so especially as they'd had no idea they would be on leave at the same time. They would lie in bed in the mornings, comparing tales of the sights they'd seen and although neither was aware of it at the time, they had on several occasions been no more than a stone's throw away from each other.

Unfortunately, Arthur's leave ended all too quickly and Ted walked with him to the station where he caught the 2.45am returning leave train to London – when would they meet again? *Would* they meet again? Yes, of course they would, as they'd faithfully promised their parents they would return home safe and sound.

On the day following Arthur's departure, Ted took his bicycle by train to Melton Mowbray and then rode the nine miles to his adopted village of Buckminster, to renew acquaintances with the many friends he'd made there.

Staying with Mr and Mrs George Grice for a couple of nights, it was only natural that the two men would at some time pay a visit to the Dysart Arms in the village and also to the Blue Dog at Sewstern.

It was at the latter that Ted bumped into an old mate, Bill Gibson. Bill was a member of the Saddle-Room gang at Lincoln racecourse but had suffered quite badly in the German gas attack on the Menin Road at Ypres in December 1915. He had also been in the attack on The Bluff, before submitting to severe wounds in the first Somme battle.

It was only natural that Bill wished to be remembered to everyone in 'B' Company, but as Ted sadly explained, very few of them were still around.

.....................................

Returning to Market Harborough, Ted spent his few remaining days with his parents and sister Eadie. When the time came for him to return to 'hell let loose' he was extremely reluctant to do so, but of course, he still had a duty to perform for King and Country.

Once again, his mother made him promise to come home in one piece, and she told him she also prayed every day for her other three boys who were serving in France and Belgium to do likewise.

The Old Grammar School in Market Harborough,
where troops home on leave from the Western
Front would congregate and discuss the horrors
of trench warfare

# CHAPTER 23
## Raiding Party

Having completed his final farewells, Ted slung his rifle over his shoulder and set off to catch the 2.45am London-bound train. Packed with sleeping troops returning from further north it quickly gathered speed, before eventually steaming into St Pancras. Here, the mass exodus commenced, before the men were able to board awaiting army lorries, ready to take them across the capital to Victoria Station, where other trains were queuing to take them onwards to Folkestone.

Crossing the Channel to Boulogne, almost every regiment in the British Army was represented. Silence descended upon the heaving mass, as no doubt their thoughts were with the loved ones they'd all left behind; or perhaps they were contemplating 'the road to hell on earth' upon which they would once again be travelling very soon.

Disembarking at Boulogne, all men were marched to waiting trains, each alphabetically labelled depending upon which direction the men were heading. Ted boarded train 'C' which, when full, would be on its way to the Doullens area.

Shortly after daybreak, Warlincourt was reached and all men belonging to the 17th Division alighted. Each smaller regimental unit, which helped form part of the 17th was then separated and marched to their individual billets. Lads of the 7th Lincolns were sent to Pommera again, ultimately arriving at the same farm where they had been resting up before going on leave.

Surviving the horrific shellings which decimated the 51st TMBs, when setting up their individual gun batteries alongside the Scarpe, Ted and his handful of colleagues wondered what lay in store. Previously they had been notified that their OC, Captain Squires, was on leave in Blighty, but they assumed that by now he would have returned to duty. Subsequently they anticipated news as to their immediate future with the TMBs.

Within the next three days, the Captain still hadn't put in an appearance, so all men concerned received instructions from the CO, Lieutenant Colonel Metcalfe, to continue their duties as infantrymen with the 7th Lincolns until told otherwise.

The very next day, the 7th were instructed to join up with other units of the 17th Division, as they were needed to assist the 51st Brigade in the trenches between Athies and Fampoux. This meant a long march to Arras followed by a much shorter one to their final destination.

For over two and a half years, it was widely acknowledged that the Germans held the upper hand in trench warfare, but by the middle of June 1917, Tommy had perfected the art of raiding and more often than not, Hindenburg's pride and joy were forced to submit to the superiority of our valorous lads.

......................................

Entering the forward trench, the 7th were told to make themselves available to provide a raiding party of eighty men at daybreak. Those taking part were to be selected by two officers and the CSM, with practically every man hoping that he wouldn't be a recipient of the dreaded shoulder tap.

It was a beautiful morning, as the first glimpse of orange sun made itself visible over Vimy. Chosen at random, the unfortunate ones smoked a final cigarette as they awaited the order to 'go over the top'. Each one of the eighty taking part struggled to calm their nerves, as they were well aware this could well be their very last day on the earth.

Without warning, the artillery bombarded Fritz's line with their usual pinpoint accuracy, thus enabling the Poachers to cross the Scarpe without interference. In fact, the entire operation was so well synchronised that Jerry's forward line was infiltrated before he was aware of any ground attack taking place.

Jumping into the trench at varying distances, the lads charged with glistening bayonets violently thrusting forward, while at the same time screaming like the hounds of hell. Many enemy troops lost their lives that morning and a good few were taken prisoner.

Ted, Charlie Wright and a couple of new lads rounded up a dozen or so very young, totally demoralised Germans, herding them like stampeding cattle towards the Scarpe. Panic-stricken, they waded across and spurred on by their captors, they dropped into the Lincolns' trench, still with hands held high. Feeling sorry for them, the lads gave them cigarettes and water. They looked so young and forlorn, causing Ted to think they should still be at school.

One of the Germans who appeared to speak a little English suddenly said "war no good" – this being a philosophical ideology which every Tommy in hearing distance wholeheartedly endorsed.

Such attacks, of course, did not take place without casualties on the British side too, and on this occasion, a third of the raiding party failed to return. Nevertheless, the end result was deemed worthy to justify the means and the cost, or at least it was at GHQ, but those sturdy lads from Lincolnshire thought otherwise.

During a lull in hostilities, less than two days after the raid, a small group of survivors huddled together in the trench, quietly discussing the rights and wrongs of such incursions, each one of them voicing opinions in a highly critical manner. The high-ranking 'whisky guzzlers' at GHQ who were responsible for such crackpot strategy came in for special condemnation, and no doubt if any one of them appeared before a trench Tommy's Kangaroo Court, he would have been sent before a firing squad.

Ted made it abundantly clear that he did not volunteer to fight for King and Country, in order to bayonet-charge young teenagers and the rest of the gathering were in full agreement.

Over several months, the lads in the line had become increasingly critical of their officers' conduct. As their Saps

became increasingly more like small bungalows, furnished with proper beds, tables, chairs and even carpets, all pillaged from ruined houses, it was becoming more of a rarity to see an officer directing operations within the trenches.

Officially Tommy was not allowed alcohol while on line duty, but it rankled when he found out just how many bottles of whisky and the like were being smuggled into the Saps under cover of darkness.

It was claimed that the reason why officers drank so much was to steady their nerves. However, Tommy also suffered from nerves which needed steadying, but as he was considered to be of inferior status, he was regarded as being undeserving of any form of stimulus.

Many of the replacement officers were still in their late teens and they'd obviously received their commissions because of family prominence or superior educational background. The sergeant majors ran things in the line and more often than not, these credulous young men would ask them what was to be done. But of course, this was the British Army and the nepotism of the old-school-tie network took precedence over everything.

.....................................

After sixteen days in the line, the 17th Division was relieved and it was a return to the austere St Nicholas Camp. Every soldier, irrespective of regiment, who spent time in the place absolutely loathed it, although to compensate the Arras nightlife was utopia by comparison.

Returning French civilians were reaping a rich harvest from the thousands of troops stationed in or around Arras. Homes and shops were hastily renovated and restored to supply their every need.

The city centre was still a total wreck, but in streets adjacent to the Square, shops sold almost every commodity imaginable. For Tommy there was a YMCA, cinemas, theatre et cetera and naturally there were estaminets, which were always well patronised. In fact, it was fast becoming like Armentières – welcoming and pleasurable.

"Dawn Raiding Party"

# CHAPTER 24

## Horatio Bottomley

The 17th Division's period of activity in the Arras Sector had come to an unexpected close, with the 7th Lincolns being ordered to await fresh instructions. It was during this interval that Ted celebrated three years of army service; three years which seemed more like thirty-three.

Such a varied amount of happenings had arisen since that early morning cycle ride along the Great North Road, when the three Buckminster lads travelled to Grantham Barracks to enlist for the duration. What began as a thrilling adventure, turned out to be anything but, with the hard truth of reality being immeasurably more horrifying than ever the human mind could possibly have conceived.

Whatever went wrong with all those deluded newspaper headlines which predicated it would all be over by Christmas? Unfortunately, they omitted to say which Christmas…

...........................................

Queuing for breakfast one morning at St Nicholas Camp, Ted accidentally bumped into the third member of that carefree cycling group, his pal of pre-war days, Tom Armstrong.

Such a vast amount of water had fiercely passed beneath the proverbial bridge since their last meeting, but how excessively exuberant they were to see each other again. For some reason or other, Tom's officer had transferred to the Durham Light Infantry and, of course, it was only natural for his groom to go with him.

With so much to talk about, the two mates arranged to meet up in one of the most popular army-patronised estaminets in Arras that same evening and what an evening it turned out to be.

Along with a trio of old 'B' Company pals from racecourse days – Alf Letts, Tom Weller and Arthur Atter, Ted and Tom recalled old friends and old times, and they toasted each other's health and happiness as only Tommy knew how. Each one continually maintaining they weren't really cut out for a soldier's life.

As the evening wore on, a small group of West Ridings (9th Duke of Wellingtons Regiment) entered the room and Ted suddenly heard his name being called out. Turning to see who it was, he was again overjoyed to see yet another old mate, whom he knew when working for a short while in Yorkshire. Walter Spenceley was employed on the very same country estate, Broughton Hall near Skipton, and the pair of them had formed a firm friendship.

Under normal circumstances, the two of them may never have set eyes upon each other ever again, but a world war and military service had, by pure chance, brought them together in an estaminet in Arras. So one could only imagine just how many more times that evening glasses were raised to wish each other the very best of health.

......................................

During the few remaining days at St Nicholas Camp, it was quite amazing just how many old pals Ted unexpectedly encountered, and more often than not, in the oddest of places.

One warm Sunday morning, for instance, Ted went with several Lincolnshire lads to the swimming baths to cool off, and lo and behold who should tap him on the shoulder when in the water, but an old Market Harborough mate by the name of Ernie Richardson. Ted and Ernie attended the same school and afterwards they became keen members of the same gymnasium in the town.

Having walked to St Aubin, on an errand for Lieutenant Radley, Ted was starting out on the return journey, when thumbing a lift with an army limber. He was staggered to find the driver was another old school pal by the name of Archie Bosworth. Needless to say, they pulled up outside the very first estaminet they came across and celebrated the occasion over a bottle of vin blanc.

........................................

One day at St Nicholas, the camp was visited by the celebrated *Daily Mail* columnist, Horatio Bottomley. Officers, NCOs and Tommies alike, all loved to read his articles and they lost precious little time in telling him so. But when he returned to Fleet Street afterwards, he began almost every sentence of his articles with the words "I have." It was, "I have been to Arras"... "I have been to Athies"... "I have been observed by the enemy"... "I have been shelled"... "I have been in a trench"... "I have been close to a German." Etc, etc, etc. Now Tommy being Tommy, he simply couldn't stop laughing at what Horatio had written. All the lads had spent weeks on end in Arras, which by the way was one of the quietest sectors on the Western Front. *They'd* been in Athies umpteen times; *they'd* been observed by the enemy more times than Mr Bottomley had had hot dinners! *They'd* been one of a dozen or so front-line men who'd shaved at the very same time from cold water in the very same tin hat. *They'd* been shelled more times than any of them could possibly remember, and as for being in a trench, the lads didn't just pop into one for a couple of minutes then scarper; *they* had lived in them, ate their lousy bully in them, slept in them, shot at Fritz thousands of times from them, and witnessed the sight of their own mates being blown to kingdom come in them. As for being close to just one German, the lads had been close to thousands upon thousands – and yes they'd even answered the call of nature in them.

But then again it was as Tommy said, "Don't worry about it mate, with a bit of luck, it might all be over by Christmas."

# CHAPTER 25

## Return to Flanders

At last it was time for the 17th Division to take their leave of the Arras Sector, and move back to Flanders, where they were to join the 2nd Army's 'Big Push'.

The early morning journey began with a twenty-kilometre march to Liencourt via Warlus, Wanguetin and Avesnest-le-Zomte. Surprisingly, the lads spent a whole week here, making friends with local people in their cottages and small holdings, before some simpleton spoilt it all by ordering them to pack up and proceed to Belgium.

Saulty railhead was the first port of call, after which it was yet another of those slow uncomfortable cattle-truck-type journeys to Proven, midway between Berques and Ypres. Staying overnight at a camp called Shooter's Hill, the division departed for the village of Sint Juliaan, where they were designated to relieve a guard's division, only to be relieved themselves a mere eight hours later.

"I say there, what the bloody hell is going on?" demanded the officers. "What soddin' idiot's responsible for this friggin balls-up?" the CSMs wished to know.

Tommy, however, put it a little more inelegantly. Sent back to Shooter's Hill for the remainder of the day, the lads were later taken on what seemed like a typical Army wild-goose chase, to a place by the name of Elverdinge, a few kilometres north-west of Ypres. They had been messed about a bit during the previous few days, and once more, Tommy's no-frills verbal approach to the unsatisfactory situation was completely lacking any kind of refinement. In fact, to the average disgruntled infantryman, all the moving from pillar to post was completely unnecessary, and even more so as it was raining cats and dogs at the time.

....................................

On the night of October 11th 1917, positions were taken up in front-line trenches, each man having with him one hundred and twenty rounds of ammunition, as well as sufficient rations to take him through at least eight hours of fighting, which was scheduled to commence at daybreak.

Field guns were due to get the action underway with a barrage of accurate firing, immediately followed by a rapid infantry advance.

The bombardment was almost beyond belief, with gun flashes illuminating a large area where Langemark once stood, until levelled by attacks and counter-attacks.

Standing knee-deep in twenty-four carat Flanders' mud, the gunners maintained a constant onslaught, although Fritz gradually began to respond.

Ground conditions for such an assault were typical of the Ypres Salient, especially for the time of year –mud, mud, nothing but mud! Every shell hole was full to the brim with stinking chocolate-brown water, into which some of the lads sometimes slipped, and weighed down by heavy equipment, they were never seen alive again.

Should the attack succeed, it would be a great distinction for the Brigade and it would reflect the highest form of credit on the infantry, especially as many of the replacements would be experiencing their very first time in action.

Far-reaching lines of men belonging to different regiments stretched out across the unwelcoming plain, waterlogged by continuous rain over many days. Struggling to make progress through the squelching glue-like mire, a large amount of them became easy prey for Fritz's marksmen, their crumpled bodies falling face downward into the bubbling ooze.

Giving any form of help to a fallen comrade was completely out of the question, as time was of the essence, and in any case, self-preservation was a high priority.

Striving vigorously on toward their objective, the lads cursed everyone and everything they believed were responsible for starting wars. They wished ill upon all GHQ generals and politicians, and even God's role in the matter received some blasphemous questioning.

By the time enemy positions were reached, neither side was in a fit state to wage a full-scale battle, and Fritz, having taken considerable punishment from the artillery boys, surrendered without attempting any kind of serious resistance. As the lads remarked later, "Thank God for that, for if Jerry had locked horns and decided to scrap it out, then it might well have been our lot who packed it in."

Rumours of a great victory filtered through, with the 17th taking their objective even though numerous inexperienced replacements played a vital part in the operation. Insufficiently trained they nevertheless played a splendid role in the success.

Returning to Proven, the division was paraded before some high-ranking bigwig from GHQ, and he complimented them on their professionalism and the magnificent job they'd carried out under extremely difficult circumstances. But of course, Tommy being Tommy, he wasn't fooled by such pretentious mealy-mouthed clap-trap. Standing at ease next to Ted was Alf Letts, who sarcastically retorted, "Blah, blah, bloody blah

163

– what bloody insincere bunkum." And shortly afterwards he followed it up with, "What in God's name does that bloody clown know about difficult circumstances? You've only got to look at the size of his fat belly, fat arse and highly polished boots to know that he's never had to struggle through anything in his entire life, other than a six-course dinner!"

The condescending so-called big shot, who was bedecked with more medal ribbons than a complete regiment of trench Tommies, went on to mention how delighted headquarters were with the outcome of the attack, yet made no reference whatsoever to those splendid young men who'd paid the ultimate price in order that his fellow brass-hats could gloat about their great victory, to any other whisky-swiggers who happened to be in earshot.

..........................................

Back in Blighty, it seemed the recruiting campaign was not as successful as it had been during the earlier years, when all patriotic young men went willingly to do their duty for King and Country.

Over a period of time, news from the front began to be published in far greater detail by the British press and this often caused an adverse effect on enrolment figures. For if the would-be recruits were able to read that the cream of Britain's youth were being slaughtered on a large scale daily, then who could blame them for thinking that names like Somme Sector or Ypres Salient should be steered well clear of. Belgium and France were certainly reaping a bountiful supply of our finest and would continue to do so for the foreseeable future.

My God, what a death toll this struggle for supremacy was creating. What a monstrous graveyard for the flower of British manhood.

Newspaper columnists wrote glowingly of the prowess of our unbeatable regiments, while seemingly overlooking the hideous price being paid in human life.

| Alf | Ernie | Arthur |
|-----|-------|--------|
| Letts | Edwards | Skins |

**Three good mates who served together almost throughout the entire war**

# CHAPTER 26
## The Road to Passchendaele

Having made themselves comfortable – or as comfortable as possible under the circumstances – the 7th Lincolns were suddenly moved from Shooter's Hill to Priestwood Camp, just off the Poperinge Road.

Under canvas in a large damson orchard, the lads took it for granted that all the fruit belonged to them, even more so as it was well into the middle of October, which was considered to be way beyond the recognised gathering season. Unfortunately, the owners didn't quite see it that way, for within next to no time, they'd put in a claim to GHQ for loss of crop. The CO received a reprimand from higher authority and within twenty-four hours of the dastardly crime being reported, a posse of military policemen arrived to investigate.

Tommy being Tommy was in no mood to worry about some nonsensical interrogation and he delighted in telling the inquisitors just what they could do with their questions. The matter was referred to the officers, and they too made it abundantly clear that, as far as they were concerned, the issue was being blown up out of all proportion. Taking the hint that their intrusion wasn't welcome, the MPs mounted their horses and rode off, not wishing to cause further unnecessary tasks for themselves, as well as having no desire to humiliate any of the lads who'd spent so much time in the line.

......................................

For some weird and wonderful reason, it seemed as if the Poachers were suddenly being treated with a little more consideration, as they were told to make themselves ready to go further into the French countryside for an extended rest period. Although suspicious of the motive, the 7th were, nevertheless, highly delighted, and Tommy not being one to look a gift-horse in the mouth, was up at the crack of dawn, laughing and joking like youngsters waiting to go on a day trip to Cleethorpes.

Washing and shaving in readiness for a much earlier breakfast than usual, an even greater shock was in store when a convoy of London-style buses, with the words 'London Omnibus Company' printed on their sides, were parked along the road outside the camp. Immediately after all the hullabaloo calmed down, all personnel were instructed to board them.

Travelling through several villages, inhabitants stared in disbelief as most of them hadn't seen a red double-decker before, and if the truth was known, neither had quite a few of the lads who were passengers.

Coming to a halt in the small town of Licques, men and equipment were quickly unloaded, with each detachment being allocated different billets in and around the main street area. One small group, which included Ted, Arthur Perrins and Alf Letts, managed to get themselves installed in a rather cramped disused room above a cobbler's shop.

An excellent week was spent in Licques, with its estaminets and cafés doing a roaring trade. The marvellous welcome accorded them by the townsfolk was greatly appreciated, and yet again, one which the lads would remember always.

Walking along the main thoroughfare one morning, Ted was overjoyed to bump into an old friend with whom he had lost contact – Len Brewster, a Sproxton lad. Len was one of the early 'B' Company gang, but for some reason or other, they'd both been given temporary postings elsewhere. Naturally, the two of them did what all Tommies did when unexpectedly meeting up with old mates – they celebrated the occasion over a glass or three, in the first estaminet which they came upon!

Just as the lads were really enjoying their way of life, some headcase had to go and upset the applecart by ordering them to return to Belgium. Of course, as everyone knew, this meant a much speedier return to trench warfare than anticipated.

All day long, the Lincolns let it be known they were highly resentful of such back-stabbing treatment being dished out without a single 'by-your-leave,' just because some incompetent joker at GHQ had got his troop-movement calculations wrong.

Promised three weeks' prolonged rest, only to have it terminated after just one, merely confirmed what every front-line Tommy suspected. If nothing else they were expendable, and those class-prejudiced brass hats, whose only knowledge of real warfare was from what they read about in the newspapers, simply couldn't care less.

Injustice or otherwise, however, the 7th packed up bag and baggage, and returned to Proven courtesy of the good old London Omnibus Company.

........................................

Arriving at Prestwood Camp, the handful of men who had been temporarily transferred to the 51st Trench Mortar Battery, were informed that Captain Squires had now returned to active service and was doing everything in his power to resurrect his mortar-gun teams.

Joined by two dozen other volunteers from the 8th South Staffs and 10th Sherwoods, the six 7th lads who survived that horrendous day when enemy artillery decimated their gun crews, as well as their guns alongside the River Scarpe, now brought the battery up to full strength.

Ted being one of the former gun leaders, selected his five mates to be his crew, and after a further two days' refresher course, they were ready for action.

With Captain Squires in command, very ably assisted by Lieutenants Jarvis and Glen, the detachment moved out of Priestwood, being relocated slightly north of Polygon Wood, six kilometres east of Ypres. It seemed that an urgent request had been made to the 17th Division's CO for his battery of TMBs to give support to a New Zealand Division, which was involved in heavy fighting near to Zennebeke.

In consultation with the New Zealanders' front-line officers, Captain Squires arranged to set up his individual gun batteries in an agreed spot, where the Labour Corps had carried out marvellous work in clearing vast amounts of mud.

Continually pounding enemy lines for the following six hours, the TMBs enabled our gallant colonial friends to move forward through some of the worst terrain imaginable.

With a job very well done, the 51st TMB were switched to give support to the good old 17th Division, who were now back in action but bogged down in a sea of rich Flanders' ooze. Both Allied and German equipment was strewn haphazardly across several kilometres of this godforsaken eyesore, with even the odd tank gradually subsiding.

Several divisions, including Australian, Canadian, New Zealand, French, Belgium and British had been operating in this third Ypres Battle for many months, but now as the infantry battalions of each nation stretched out between Poelkappell – Westrozebake Road and the Ypres-Roulers Railway, the big prize would hopefully be Passchendaele Ridge.

For a whole week, the Germans put up stubborn resistance, but on the 10th November news filtered through to all Allied Divisions that the Canadian 1st and 2nd Divisions had finally conquered all opposition amongst the ruins of Passchendaele village.

..........................................

A vast amount of men from several nationalities gave their lives to gain this exceptional victory. Working like billy-o, those unsung heroes, the Labour Corps, removed mountains of squelching swamp-like sludge from what at one time were roads and tracks, while those incredible infantrymen carried out their horrendous assignments with the utmost skill and professionalism, often to be mown down by machine gun fire in the most frightful conditions ever known to man.

...........................................

During the course of this final Ypres Battle, which began in July 1917 and came to an agonising conclusion four months later, there were approximately 350,000 Allied casualties. Whether or not the small amount of land gained was worth it, was highly debatable, but when Sir Douglas Haig sent secret instructions to the 4th Army to withdraw from the Passchendaele Salient, little more than a month following their astonishing success, front-line Tommy openly talked of their comrades being used as gun-fodder.

This photograph shows a group of stretcher-bearers searching for dead comrades after the battle had ended.

## The Mire of Passchendaele

Heavy rain and the complete destruction by both sides' bombardment of the Flanders drainage in 1917 produced appalling conditions in which men were frequently sucked under and killed by the mud if they slipped from the duckboards.

# CHAPTER 27

## Disastrous Outcome

Having once again spent just seven days of a promised three-week rest period at Bonningues-les-Ardres, the 17th Division was ordered to pack up in readiness to move out. Infuriated, Tommy lost precious little time in letting all and sundry know exactly what he felt about the preposterous treatment he was being subjected to and the characteristic no-nonsense manner in which he made his critical analysis left no one in any doubt whatsoever of what he thought of military orders. "Just one bloody week, one friggin' lousy week," Tommy grumbled repeatedly. "I tell you mate, they treat bloody Jerry prisoners a bloody sight better than they do us lot."

After more dithering by the powers that be, final orders to depart were received just after midnight on a dark, freezing cold night in December 1917.

......................................

Returning unexpectedly from his Christmas shopping trip in Paris, Captain Squires was in time to resume command of the TMBs, with Lieutenant's Glen and Tyrell being jointly second in command. Lieutenant Radley had returned to the 8th South Staffs and was replaced by Lieutenant Jarvis of the Borders' Regiment.

Although it was destination unknown, the four officers travelled in the comparative comfort of a limber, while Tommy was to make the transference by rail.

The captain had told his batman to prepare himself for a long monotonous train journey, so everyone began to speculate as to where their destination might be.

First of all, it was a ten-kilometre march to the railhead at Wismes, then packed-in like sardines, the train slowly pulled out of the station into the dark French countryside. Standing up, it was virtually impossible to get to sleep, and if the reluctant warriors didn't get themselves squashed to death, then the awful black smoke and soot, which descended upon them in the open-topped trucks, would come close to doing Fritz's job for him.

What an appalling transit it turned out to be, taking almost two whole days to complete the sixty or so kilometre distance. Shunting and stopping in sidings as only French train drivers knew how, such luxuries as sleep, card games and even urinating was completely out of the question. Although in one secluded siding, doors were forced open and a mad uncivilized stampede ensued, as all men in the division raced towards a small leafless orchard to relieve themselves. Not a pretty sight by any stretch of the imagination.

Dawn was breaking over Mory and Sapignies, as the engine finally pulled its cargo of irritable young men towards journey's end. Yawning, disgruntled and half-frozen, they piled out onto an improvised platform some with eyes half-closed, some moaning and groaning, while others demanded to know exactly where they were and when they were going to be fed.

Bapaume was the name painted on a piece of rough wood nailed onto just about the only piece of brick wall which was still upright.

"My God," thought Ted, how the place had changed since he was last there. It used to be a flourishing town, but like so many of France's built-up settlements, it was in ruins. With very few houses still standing, it made for a pitiable sight indeed. Full of troops of many nationalities, all seemingly having no idea of when and where they were going.

Allowed a couple of hours' rest, in which they were given an example of army catering at its lowest standard, the division then marched through the ruined villages of Bancourt and Haplincourt, before reaching a place by the name of Barastre. Here they were informed that this was to be their last stopping point, or at least it was until such time as they were needed in the line. As Tommy observed in his inimitable style, there were insufficient buildings of reasonable condition to kennel a stray dog in, let alone a thousand men.

Instructed to carry on marching, they reached an abandoned camp of windswept tents, just a few hundred metres outside the village. For a few days the grumbling mass were billeted here, but six days before Christmas, the 51st TMBs were informed they were needed to relieve 141st TMBs which was a sub-division of the 47th Division, London Territorials.

Ted was told by Captain Squires to make preparations to move out as soon as possible, although Lieutenant Glen would be giving all gun leaders final details within the hour.

The guns' travelling arrangements needed to be secured, but the lads were well aware this was going to be anything but easy, as their journey would be through some of the worst shell-holed roads in France. Ted's team comprised Arthur Perrins, Charlie Wright, Tom Wood, Percy Welbourne and Jim Suckling.

On a narrow sunken road, barely a kilometre from Havrincourt, Lieutenant Glen ordered everyone to pitch tents for the night. It was an instruction which the lads treated with considerable derision and Tommy being Tommy, he couldn't restrain himself from letting the officer know exactly what he thought of such a ludicrous idea. For being told to pitch tents alongside such a disintegrated structure, and on a bitterly cold night into the bargain, the TMB crews were left spitting blood. Of course, Tommy's indelicate phraseology left much to be desired at the best of times, but whenever he was really annoyed it was hoped the padre wasn't in earshot.

During the night, Jerry's artillery gave a powerful display, in which they pinpointed every building in Havrincourt, irrespective of whether or not they had been previously targeted. Watching the demonstration from their high vantage point, Ted and his colleagues were well aware that they might well have spent the night exactly where those shells rained down. The onslaught must have killed many men, but the TMB lads could only thank whoever their God happened to be, as well as Lieutenant Glen, of course.

........................................

For two full days, the 51st TMB fired their deadly projectiles into enemy lines south of Graincourt, thus allowing the 47th to advance and occupy a vital objective.

During the early hours of Christmas Eve morning, guns fell into an eerie, almost death-like silence and Tommy wondered if it was the start of a festive-season truce, or was it just a genuine lull in activities – a lull before the storm.

It wasn't the most pleasant of mornings by a long chalk, although by ten o'clock, the rolling patches of ground mist gradually began to disperse. Sitting in a small circle drinking one of Arthur Perrin's special brews, the small gathering were discussing the previous forty-eight hours' events, when a messenger suddenly appeared amongst them from out of the blue.

Handing over a communication from Captain Squires, Lieutenant Glen glanced at its contents then slowly began to shake with laughter.

"You'll never guess in a month of Sundays what Battery HQ have done now," he said. "Some brazen buggers have hijacked their drinking water and now they've asked us to take three small drums over to them."

Water was, of course, one of those essential commodities, highly prized by everyone in the front line, and losing it was akin to any Tommy losing his rifle.

When the officer asked for three volunteers to do the necessary, Tom Wood, Percy Welbourne and Jim Suckling jumped to their feet, with one arm raised, almost like over-enthusiastic schoolboys.

Approaching 11am, the trio departed after being told by Lieutenant Glen to return as quickly as possible. Humorous comments, mostly about taking wrong turnings, sent them on their way, this being typical good-natured banter between a group of good mates.

Allowing a few minutes for the threesome to stop and chat with their mates at HQ, they were expected to be back within the hour, but when they hadn't put in an appearance by mid-afternoon, Lieutenant Glen and the other three lads became decidedly worried. At that point the officer took it upon himself to make his way to HQ in an effort to find out what was happening.

Darkness had fallen before the officer returned and he confirmed that his three missing men had left Battery HQ just before midday, although his enquiries with other trench officers and men on his way back filled him with despair, as all questions drew a blank.

Lieutenant Glen, Ted, Arthur and Charlie were still discussing their colleagues' mystifying disappearance when an almost unintelligible sound seemed to be calling out from the sinister darkness of no man's land.

Remaining perfectly still and listening with bated breath, the foursome visibly shuddered when the surreal noise was repeated, but at that very same moment in time, they all realised it was a call for help though whether or not the distressed presence was British or German was anyone's guess.

Climbing out of the trench, Lieutenant Glen asked Ted to accompany him and together they raced over to where they assumed the eerie sound was coming from and within thirty seconds they came across a severely injured Tommy, who was dragging himself at snail's pace towards British lines.

In great pain, the man was desperately trying to say something to his two rescuers, but his words were quite unintelligible.

"Just hang on in there," the Lieutenant told him, "we'll soon get you to a dressing station."

Lowering the Tommy into the awaiting arms of Arthur Perrins and Charlie Wright, they lay him down in a hole which had been dug in the side of the trench. The officer then lit a small lamp and upon inspecting the body a little more thoroughly he realised it was no other than Jim Suckling. The luck of coming across his own mates after crawling through no man's land had been purely coincidental.

Within thirty minutes, stretcher-bearers had patched up Jim and had taken him down the line for professional treatment. Lieutenant Glen accompanied them, after telling the three men to do their best until he returned.

..........................................

Christmas Day arrived, or at least some passing comedian implied that it had, when he paused to wish the indignant trio a rather high-spirited "Merry Christmas, gentlemen."

Freezing and hungry, not one of them acknowledged the lone messenger's well-meaning greeting. Although Ted did remark that he thought the half-baked so-and-so was most probably the padre in disguise. Arthur reckoned the poor chap was more to be pitied than blamed, while Charlie being Charlie merely said he was a bloody crackpot.

In any case, as everything in sight was associated with war in all its repulsive ugliness, it was extremely difficult to conjure up a vision of normal people in normal jobs, in a normal world gathering to celebrate the birthday of Jesus Christ.

..........................................

A few days after the so-called festive season, the TMBs were withdrawn from the line, and they returned to canvas billets in the ruins of Bertincourt. One of the very first things Ted, Arthur and Charlie did was to make enquiries about the well-being of Jim Suckling, but they were informed he'd been moved to a military hospital fifty kilometres away.

Learning that Tom Wood lost his life on Christmas Eve was bad enough, but to be told that Percy Welbourne never regained consciousness and died on Christmas Day morning was a real body blow.

..........................................

The detailed report into the disappearance of the trio made disturbing reading, for it seems that a simple wrong turning in difficult weather conditions took them into Graincourt instead of Havrincourt.

Graincourt was, of course, still in the hands of the enemy, but unfortunately, the three lads didn't realise their error until it was too late. With poor visibility all around, the threesome almost made their escape, but a German machine gunner had noticed their sudden about turn and opened fire. Still running like the wind, they came within a whisker of reaching some form of reasonable refuge when the marksman raised his sights a little and caught Tom Wood in the upper back region. Percy Welbourne and Jim Suckling did manage to drop into a recently made shell hole, and it was only after the pair of them had lain totally exhausted for quite some time in their temporary sanctuary that they became aware of Woody's absence.

Making a monumental effort to move, Jim called out in obvious agony, as he felt a stinging sensation across his left shoulder blade but was shocked to find a deep wound which was percolating blood. Disorientated, he hadn't even noticed that one of the machine gun bullets had penetrated his flesh, though he quickly realised that something needed to be done to stem the blood loss.

Neither of the men possessed any kind of first-aid knowledge, so it was left to Percy to rip off his shirt sleeve and make an improvised tourniquet. Wrapping it tightly around Jim's troublesome shoulder, he then told his mate to try and keep calm and that he'd do everything possible to get him safely back to British lines.

Pulling himself to the crater's rim, Percy called Jim to let him know that he could see Woody lying motionless twenty metres away, but almost in the same breath, he turned and shouted "bloody hell Jim, I reckon he's still alive."

Without hesitating to consider the implications involved, Percy clambered out of his temporary sanctuary, and accelerated towards his seriously injured colleague.

Picking up the limp body, he raced helter-skelter in the same direction from which he came, but just as the two of them were on the verge of reaching their destination, Fritz opened up again. Riddled so maliciously, Percy fell forward, his head hanging motionlessly over the crater's edge, while Woody's body shot forward on the diagonal to where Jim was watching proceedings through half-closed eyes.

Anyone who'd served King and Country for any length of time on the battlefields of France and Belgium were witness to countless deaths, more often than not in the most gruesome of circumstances, but Tommy became hardened to it. However, when the deaths were of good mates, with whom a close bond of camaraderie had been formed, it was then the mental anguish almost became unbearable.

........................................

Private Percy Welbourne, who gave his own life in trying to save the lives of his two mates, was a genuine hero.

Recommending him for the highest military honour, Captain Squires was absolutely dumbfounded when he learned the powers that be at GHQ didn't even think that such a solemn entreaty was worthy of acknowledgment. Yet they all wore rows and rows of medal ribbons and not one of them had ever been in a front line in their entire lives, let alone fought in any truly meaningful battle.

Name:   WELBOURNE, Percy

Initials:   P

Nationality:   United Kingdom

Rank:   Private

Regiment:   Lincolnshire

Unit Text:   7th Bn. Secondary
Unit Text: attd. 51st T.M.Bty

Age:   23

Date of Death:   25/12/1917

Service No:   19062

Add information:  Son of late Mr
G & Mrs F Welbourne of 8 New
Row, Gonerby Hill Foot,
Grantham

Casualty Type:   Commonwealth
War Dead

Grave/Memorial Reference: Bay
3 & 4

Cemetery: ARRAS MEMORIAL

What a devastating Christmas Percy's nearest and dearest would have back home in Grantham. Aged just 23 he was another fine son of England, who would never again hear a dawn chorus in woodlands surrounding his home, or be able to listen to Grantham Parish Church bells on a Sunday evening.

Private Thomas Wood was an 8th Battalion South Staffs' man, but moved over to the 51st TMBs for what he hoped would be a much quieter life. Unfortunately, that quieter life ended horrifically on the back of one of his best mates, in a freezing cold foreign field on Christmas Eve, 1917.

**Name: WOOD, Thomas**

Initials: T

Nationality: United Kingdom

Rank: Private

Regiment: South Staffordshire

Unit Text: 8th Bn.

Date of Death: 24/12/1917

Service No: 22150

Casualty Type: Commonwealth War Dead

Grave/Memorial Reference: Bay 6

Cemetery: ARRAS MEMORIAL

Private James Suckling was born and bred in Great Waltham, Essex but for some reason, known only to himself, he chose the 1st Battalion, Lincolns at the time of enlistment. An invaluable member of the 51st TMBs, it was due to his honest appraisal of Percy Welbourne's courageous acts that inspired Captain Squires to recommend Percy for the highest award.

The severity of Jim's wounds meant that he was sent back to Blighty. No further information was forthcoming and as far as the lads were aware, he did not return to active service.

Name: SUCKLING, James

Initials: J

Nationality: United Kingdom

Rank: Private

Regiment: Lincolnshire

Unit Text: 1st Bn.

Age: 21

Date of Death: 16/04/1918

Service No: 51651

Add information: Son of James and Hannah Suckling of Wisemass, Great Waltham, Chemlsford, Essex

Casualty Type: Commonwealth War Dead

Grave/Memorial Reference: Panel 35 to 37 and 162 to 162A

Cemetery: TYNE COT MEMORIAL

It later transpired that James Suckling did, in fact, return to active service but sadly lost his life on 16th April 1918 (see page 220)

# CHAPTER 28

## Them and Us

With the 7th Battalion being in the line over the Christmas period, headquarters decided to give the lads a feast fit for a King's banquet.

Facilities were arranged, whereby a large amount of pork, with practically every other ingredient needed to make an out-of-the-ordinary meal, was purchased in Amiens. Lorries were despatched to collect generous supplies, including Christmas puddings, barrels of beer and bottles galore of best quality French wines. Cigars and cigarettes were also on the shopping list and how grateful the lads were. What a tremendous difference in army policy it all was.

Opening their Christmas mail, they were feeling blissfully exuberant to receive cards, letters and parcels from loved ones back home. Ted was fortunate enough to be included on two 'Funds for Soldiers' lists. One of these was from his home town of Market Harborough, who sent a ten-shilling note and three pairs of hand-knitted socks, while his adopted village of Buckminster sent a £1 note. Both were marvellous surprises and extremely welcome.

.........................................

While still in Bertincourt, Ted again bumped into his old Buckminster pal Tom Armstrong, and it was only natural that they spend a quiet afternoon together discussing snippets of news received from various friends in the village they so loved.

Most divisions had their very own concert party and the 17th was no exception. 'The Duds' by name, were exceptionally talented and performing in an improvised canteen, Ted and Tom, in the company of Arthur Atter, Horace Hawley and Harold Stokes, survivors from Lincoln racecourse days, laughed along with a great many others at their highly professional production. At the close of a satisfactory day, Ted and Tom shook hands and went their separate ways, both vowing to meet up again in the not-too-distant future, preferably in their old jobs back home.

Not destined to stay too long in Bertincourt, the 17th moved out on the 3rd January 1918, with orders to relieve both the 47th and 2nd Divisions – and what a night that was too.

It was pitch black and ice cold with freezing snow attacking Tommy's unprotected face, like bullets at fifty paces. Just walking was a nightmare, causing the lads to slip and slither like a herd of bullocks in a sea of mud, while being harassed by the farmer's collie.

Nearing the Canal du Nord, at a point known to all Allied troops as 'Slag Heap', a warning signal was received by all senior officers, confirming that the Germans had counter-attacked – although at the time it was unclear as to whether or not it was on a large scale.

Enemy artillery certainly had a bee in its bonnet, as shells were exploding indiscriminately without respite, though in next to no time, our own gunners were answering back.

When making a direct hit on the canal bank some two weeks earlier, a howitzer shell completely emptied it, thus leaving the waterway bottom frozen hard. This, in turn, allowed both troops and certain types of motorised transport to move along it quite easily.

Beneath wrecked bridges they walked, all the time silently praying to their maker not to let Fritz land one of his deadly missiles amongst them. Another guide then directed the lads towards the line, while the six mortar crews were sent to operate from the far end of a narrow trench close by.

Captain Squires had made the crossing to Blighty for the New Year, which meant that Lieutenant Glen was temporarily in command. Straightaway, he was installed in a Sap originally built by enemy troops, before retreating at the time of the 3rd Army's 'Big Push'. Typical of German creativity, it was fully furnished, and according to the lieutenant's servant, it was well stocked with crates galore of all kinds of spirits and best quality wines.

Unfortunately, Tommy had no such luxury to keep him warm and protected from the dreadful elements. Expected to give maximum effort and performance at all times, minor details such as severe weather conditions, which not only froze men's fingers and toes but sometimes froze them to death, were not accepted as an excuse for falling below standards. Standards set by those faceless wonders at GHQ who had never set eyes on a trench, let alone spent weeks at a stretch living, fighting and dying in one.

Waiting for three whole days and nights, Tommy was in a state of nervous uncertainty, continually anticipating the imminent arrival of Hindenburg's hordes, but nothing out of the ordinary happened. However, all wasn't too quiet, as shells continued to explode all around them. Sometimes they killed and sometimes they maimed, or failing that they merely enlarged the thousands of craters made by both sides in the conflict, days, weeks or even months beforehand.

Just before dawn broke on the following Sunday –at least Tommy assumed it was Sunday, although he wasn't too sure about it – the lads began to wonder where the dripping sound was coming from. At the time, none of them realised it was the first signs of a thaw setting in. Nevertheless, within the hour, there was mud galore oozing into the trench and it was becoming progressively worse by the minute.

Walking was virtually impossible, so in their desperation the lads hacked out platforms to sit on, near to the parapet. Extreme pressure eventually caused the trench rear wall to collapse and immediately masses of brown porridge-like slush gushed away like water leaving canal locks after its gates are opened. In fact, so horrendous had the situation become that ropes had been hurriedly fastened to hastily erected fencing stakes along the ridge to enable Tommy to move without fear of slipping into what would have been a certain death.

No food supplies were able to get through. Subsequently rations were desperately short. Enemy snipers were conspicuous by their absence, so it was fairly obvious that they too were struggling to cope in identical conditions.

It took almost a fortnight to rebuild the trench, but of course, the very same must have applied to Fritz. Neither side was able to bring their heavy guns into action, as any form of movement in the swamp-like conditions was totally out of the question. It was virtually impossible to move the mortars, and even if they'd been able to do so, there still would have been no chance of finding a solid piece of ground to stand them on.

On the 26th of the month, every man in the 17th received orders to sleep with his equipment on, while boots were not to be removed under any circumstance. Such an order was regarded as being a rather sick joke, for as Tommy remarked, "if the Duds Concert Party ever used such idiotic bunkum in their repertoire, the audience would have been rolling in the aisles", as none of the lads could ever remember being able to remove their footwear when in the line.

It seems the reason given for issuing such a hare-brained order was due to the fact that the following day was the Kaiser's birthday, and military intelligence (whatever that was) thought it more than likely that Fritz would stage a spectacular all-out attack to celebrate it. As it turns out, it was nothing but assumption on the part of the so-called experts at GHQ who had nothing better to do with their time.

Obviously, the Germans weren't stupid enough to launch an offensive while ground conditions were so atrocious. But of course, Tommy being Tommy, he took such simple-minded cock-ups in his stride, passing them off with derisory remarks such as, "you couldn't really expect military intelligentsia to know anything about ground conditions, now could you?"

Still debating the order in the confines of a bitterly cold, wet trench, it was unanimously agreed that whoever the high-ranking dimwit was who instigated such a mindless plan of action, most likely did so in the comfort of his family's drawing room, when he was home on leave during the Christmas period.

Tommy had no time whatsoever for the GHQ generals and tended to mimic them at every opportunity. On this particular occasion, it was Frank Waterton who set the ball rolling with, "How awfully courageous, what?.... Deserves a DSO, old boy." Whereas Charlie Wright, who probably disliked the officer class more than anyone in the entire British Army, responded with,

"Good God, my dear chap, he's already got three and hasn't been within fifty miles of the line."

...................................

Taking stock of life, Ted began to realise more than ever before that he was living on borrowed time. Officers had been killed, NCOs had been killed and Tommies had been killed in unbelievable numbers, yet here he was without a scratch on him. He'd lived side by side with death for so long, and still a bullet or shell didn't have his name on it, while some of Britain's finest sons fell on their very first day in the line.

...................................

Some member battalions of the 17th Division, including the 7th Lincolns and 51st TMBs had been in the front line for twenty-four days. So much for Haig's propositional calculus whereby troops were only to remain at the battle-front for short spells.

The exodus of the great unwashed trudged into the night, dodging around water-filled shell-craters before reaching billets known as Saunders camp, close to Haplincourt. Hoping to be able to take a long hot bath, followed by a complete change of clothing before going to sleep for at least a month, Ted and five other gun-team leaders were staggered to receive orders from Captain Squires to report to his office at once. Totally disillusioned, the six of them reached their CO's office just as Lieutenants Glen and Tyrrel were leaving.

Being after midnight, the lads were rather surprised to find the captain in full dress uniform, with both valise and carrying-case packed, although the thing which struck them most of all was that he now had the military cross ribbon pinned on his jacket.

It was, of course, a well-known fact that all commanding officers received decorations in turn, as somehow it wasn't regarded as being appropriate for one occupying such a position, if having no ribbons on show. And this unwritten ruling applied whether or not an officer had served in the line.

Congratulating the six of them on carrying out such an excellent job under the most difficult conditions, the captain then presented each one with a bottle of scotch and asked them to make sure their crews had a drink on him. Then in what almost seemed like an afterthought, he casually mentioned that he'd be away from the 51st for a month, although he conveniently neglected to say why. Coming to attention and saluting like the good subordinates they were, the six of them merely replied "thank you sir".

......................................

Lying in their makeshift beds and sipping the CO's whisky, Ted and Charlie Wright quietly analysed events of the recent past and, as so often happened, the conversation involved the role of officers.

Not unlike the majority of front-line Tommies, Charlie held a deep seated resentment of all officers, whereas Ted was less contemptuous. Charlie argued that he'd yet to come across an officer who knew much about trench warfare, while Ted reckoned that those who did were worth their weight in gold.

"Well as far as I am concerned, it's the CSMs who run the show, as most officers stay put in their cosy Saps, when the going gets rough," complained Charlie. "And what's more, it's always Tommy who does the donkey work, with no thanks whatsoever, yet it's always the men with pips on their shoulders who receive the honours."

Acknowledging that Charlie had a valid point, Ted recognised that every Tommy in the British Army resented the 'you scratch my back, I'll scratch yours policy'. It really was the class system at its worst.

Over a long period of time, both men agreed they had witnessed a great many acts of exceptional bravery, which were above and beyond the call of duty, but as all of them were performed by common 'gun fodder' Tommies or NCOs, nothing further was ever heard of them. It really was as Tommy so often remarked, "if an officer put his head out of the Sap before ten o'clock in the morning to check the weather, then you could bet a pound to a penny he'd receive a mention in dispatches."

Charlie agreed officers were necessary but couldn't bring himself to accept they should live in far superior conditions than Tommy. "The buggers get better food, better drinks and a bloody sight more of it," he moaned. "And what's more, tell me why they get six times as much leave as us silly sods do?"

Slipping slowly away into dreamland, Ted silently remembered Lieutenants Hayward and Shankster, two excellent officers whose enormous contribution to the cause eventually cost them their lives. No recognition for their lion-hearted heroism, just rough wooden crosses with their names carved on them.

There were several others too who carried out their duties bravely and conscientiously. However, it wasn't the young officers who were to blame for having better conditions or considerably more leave than Tommy – it was the system. An unjust system which caused great friction amongst the rank and file, at a time when everyone should have been committed to a common endeavour.

# CHAPTER 29

## Blighty Again

The year 1918 was moving along apace, although nothing out of the ordinary had occurred for some little while. Adverse weather conditions hadn't helped matters, but then, of course, this always affected both sets of adversaries.

Since the end of January, the Lincolns had been doing six days in the line, then six days in support in the Bertincourt area. During this time, rumours persisted about Jerry's potential 'Big Push' being imminent, up until such time as no one believed a word of it. In fact, it was as Charlie Wright who so aptly put it – "If the bastards were going to come, then they'd a-bin here months since." And you know what? Irrespective of rank everyone was in full agreement.

...................................

Returning to their undesirable billets, Ted, Charlie Boon, Charlie Wright and Corporal Bachelor were informed that they were each due for ten days' leave in Blighty.

The following day, all four were on the leave-boat bound for Folkestone. Then, it was the usual mad rush for northbound trains heading towards their nearest and dearest.

Home again; no one can begin to imagine exactly what that means, unless of course, they themselves have stood face to face with death on so many occasions, often under dreadful bombardment, each minute expecting to be sent to eternity. Then, of course, there are those beautiful words which only a mother can greet a returning son with, words which are far too sacred to divulge to any other living soul.

Ted was one of five brothers who had served in France and Belgium, though now only four of them were alive.

Not unlike millions of other parents worldwide, Ted's mother and father were totally devastated by their son Frank's death, but whereas his mother put on a very brave face for the sake of the family, it was nevertheless noticeable that she hadn't yet come to terms with the feeling of dark despair at the thought of never again being able to see him or hold him in her arms. To her, Frank was still the young, happy-go-lucky boy she had brought into this world. Meanwhile, father's health was in rapid decline and giving great cause for concern.

Most probably for the very first time, Ted realised that a war-zone death wasn't only about the loss of one life, which in itself was heartbreaking, but also of the appalling knock-on effect which caused such deep-rooted torment to the victim's loved ones.

…………...………………..

Walking through Market Harborough town centre the following morning, Ted bumped into so many people with whom he was acquainted, that not only did he find their conversation pieces to be rather hilarious but also therapeutic as they diverted his thoughts from the feeling of anguish at home.

One particular lady of maturing years asked him if he knew her youngest sister's son as she'd knitted a couple of pairs of socks for him, and wondered if it would be possible for Ted to deliver them to him. She then paused a moment before adding, "he's in the Northamptonshire regiment, you know".

Explaining that he didn't know the lad and that he had no idea where the Northants were serving, she immediately responded with, "Well, you should know – he's in France, same as you!"

Another elderly lady said she was thinking of knitting a balaclava for her grandson, who was also serving on the Somme, but told Ted she couldn't make up her mind about the colour. Imagining just what the lad's CSM would have to say if her grandson turned up in the line with a scarlet or orange garment covering his ears, he advised her to knit it in regulation khaki, otherwise the censor might well keep it for himself.

A quite well-known ostentatious man about town told Ted all about the dreadful conditions which 'our boys' were having to endure on the Western Front, and almost in the same breath added, "I bet you're jolly glad that you're not out there, aren't you son?" Ted didn't bother to enlighten him.

A week was spent at home, knocking his father's neglected garden into shape, as well as visiting several old familiar haunts. Then it was off to Melton Mowbray by train followed by a bicycle ride to Buckminster. Early morning cloud was beginning to break up, thereby allowing the sun's pallid rays to filter through roadside trees.

The many villages en route were beautifully serene for the time of year, such a far cry from those in the battle regions of France and Belgium. There were no exploding shells, no continuous detonation of machine guns or crackle of rapid rifle fire to frighten the living daylights out of the livestock, which grazed contentedly in nearby green fields, while wild birds of every description went about their early spring ritual of nest site-seeking, completely unhindered.

Leaning upon a wooden five-barred field gate close to the little school, midway between the small villages of Garthorpe and Coston, Ted listened to the laughter of young children as they played hopscotch and snobs in the playground. What a striking difference to the distressing existence which youngsters were forced to endure in every battle-scarred area from Ypres to the Somme and beyond.

Surveying the landscape from horizon to valley below, the River Eye delicately meandered between tall horse chestnuts, while groups of newly born lambs gambolled close by.

Taking everything in, Ted silently wished that such an appealing view would never ever be annihilated by the ravages of war.

Riding into Buckminster, a sudden shower caught him unawares, but it didn't make a scrap of difference to how he felt, for at that moment in time, he knew that he was entering the loveliest place on God's earth.

...................................

Back in Market Harborough, Ted was in the Working Men's Club with his father, when his attention was called to a report in the *Leicester Mercury* which confirmed the long-awaited 'German Push' had finally commenced. It seemed the initial assault began with a far greater artillery bombardment than usual, before Ludendorff's combat troops were let off the leash to carry out his boast to push the British back into the sea, from whence they came.

...................................

A quick glance at the morning newspapers when changing trains in London was sufficient to confirm that the 17th Division was in the thick of the fighting on the Cambrian Front, where the offensive began.

The four lads of the 51st TMB who had crossed the channel to England were then in high spirits, but on the return journey they were greatly subdued, knowing that very shortly they would be bound for a life of living hell, where death and mutilation were dealt out indiscriminately.

**The Dysart Arms (now the Tollemache Arms) in Main Street, Buckminster where Ted spent some of his leave**

# CHAPTER 30
## Another Lucky Escape

Slipping into Boulogne harbour, the heavily laden boat's cargo changed rapidly from their self-imposed silence to a babble of repartee.

Upon disembarkation, a vociferous CSM came out of the shadows and yelled at the top of his voice, "All men of the 17th and 41st Divisions this way! At the double."

One night was spent in Marlborough Camp on the outskirts of Boulogne, then shortly after daybreak, all men of the two divisions boarded the usual open-top train for an all-day journey to a place by the name of Puchevillers, fifteen kilometres north of Amiens. Here they alighted and marched to Warloy-Baillon, which was just a short distance from Albert.

Upon arrival, the group found nothing but chaos. No one seemed to have the slightest idea where either division was likely to be going, so tired out, they found an empty barn in the village and very soon they all fell fast asleep.

Just before cock-crow, a messenger arrived with a communication instructing the lads belonging to the 17th to make their way to Lincolnshire Transport, which they were informed was no more than a couple of kilometres away. Once there, they were allowed to wash and shave, then given breakfast before being despatched to Sailly-Saillisel, where both the 7th Lincolns and 51st TMBs were 'dug in', following their big retreat after the heroic battle to hold on to Hermies, where they'd been garrisoned. Against all odds, the battle-weary lads had fallen back in

198

order to keep in touch with their flanks, otherwise the whole lot of them would have been totally annihilated.

At Sailly, one of Ted's mates gave him first-hand information about the enemy assault, which so many had predicted would never take place. Fritz, it seemed, was believed to be too weak to be able to carry out any form of attack, but the large amount of casualties sustained by several of our own regiments was proof positive that this wasn't the case.

Many courageous deeds were performed by very ordinary young men from almost every town and village in Lincolnshire, as well as quite a few who were born over the county border, but who'd chosen to serve under the 'Poacher's' flag.

Reports came in of men being blown to smithereens by the ferocity of the enemy's constant artillery bombardment. In a great many instances, bodies were completely unidentifiable. Shelled during the day and bombed by aeroplanes at night, it had been horror and confusion at its worst. So fast and furious was the German assault that the depleted British Divisions were completely taken by surprise.

.............................

Helping to reinforce a dilapidated trench at Sailly-Saillisel, Ted experienced one of his closest encounters with death. Bending over to pick up an old piece of heavy wood, he suddenly heard a high-pitched screaming noise in front of him, immediately followed by a blinding flash and ear-splitting explosion, no more than forty metres behind him. Fragments of wood and mud flew in all directions, while Ted was sent hurtling a dozen metres into what he thought at the time was oblivion.

Regaining his senses, Ted slowly realised that had he not bent over to pick up the piece of wood at that precise moment in time, then the particular shell in question would have blown a hole right through his body, big enough to drive a tank through. What an escape he'd had, and it meant his name and number still hadn't appeared on the Angel of Death's shopping list.

# CHAPTER 31

## Death and Pandemonium

Confirmed reports of remarkable acts of courage by our men in beleaguered Hermies, continued to circulate amongst those who'd survived, and after analysing all aspects, it became evident that the tremendous resistance offered by the 7th Lincolns, 10th Sherwoods and 6th Dorsetshires greatly facilitated the safe withdrawal of other battalions.

Many weird and wonderful excuses were propounded by our so-called tactical experts in an effort to justify the Allies' failure to hold Ludendorff's attackers, but when everything was taken into consideration, the real reason stuck out like a sore thumb. In plain English, we'd taken the enemy for granted – an inexcusable blunder.

Following a winter's preparations and knowing an attack was widely predicted, far superior measures should have been implemented. The fact that this wasn't so merely endorsed what the average Tommy openly proclaimed about those high-ranking, desk-bound officers who preached a lot, but when it all boiled down, did absolutely nothing. No wonder other ranks always referred to them as 'them bloody smart-arsed toerags who reckon they know it all'.

Driven by force of circumstance, both Hindenburg and Ludendorff were being openly criticised back home in Germany, hence this last desperate effort.

Boasting about driving the British back into the sea, their 'Big Push' fizzled out as ever greater numbers of reserve battalions were brought into the action. And it was at this point the German troops suddenly realised it was the beginning of the end for them.

As fresh divisions took up positions at the front, so others who'd been in the thick of the fighting were relieved, and these included the 7th Lincolns and 51st TMB.

On this particular occasion, however, Ted considered himself rather fortunate, as only having returned from a 'Blighty' a few days beforehand, together with three of his mates, he had missed the worst of the fighting.

Having lost very many men during their advance, as well as having to contend with unseasonable weather, Jerry still continued to give a good account of himself. His artillery was particularly ebullient, especially when endeavouring to 'catch out' British troops as they moved to and from the line.

There was considerable confusion in the region, and the 51st TMB had retreated as far as Haplincourt, near to Bapaume, when they received orders to make their way to Grandcourt, another fifteen kilometres westward.

Resting up overnight, they received fresh instructions to continue their treacherous journey to a place by the name of Forceville, yet another ten kilometres further on, where they were told they'd be billeted for a couple of weeks or so.

Mortar-guns, unused shells and surplus equipment were being carried on limbers, as were Lieutenants Jeavrons and Clark. Meanwhile, all other ranks did what they always did; they just ran alongside. Having passed through Mailly-Maillet, the small convoy was within a kilometre of their destination when disaster struck.

With the lads seemingly in high spirits as they approached Forceville, they were compelled to come to an abrupt halt, when without warning, a blinding flash and one almighty explosion completely decimated the last but one limber and its entire crew. The cause, being a stray long-distance enemy shell, which made a direct hit on the vehicle.

Pandemonium reigned for quite some time, as all men who were close to where the missile had landed were in a severe state of shock, caused mainly by loss of vision. Four men were killed instantly and Lieutenant Jeavrons, as well as numerous other ranks, were seriously wounded one, being Charlie Boon.

Arriving on the scene of such brutal carnage, stretcher-bearers took control of what could only be described as a horrifying situation. They did all they could to reassure the wounded that everything was going to be all right, and that in next to no time they would be in a military hospital, where they could expect the best attention possible. Rapidly, they covered the eyes of those suffering from loss of sight, while at the same time promising them that it was only a temporary misfortune.

The tragedy caused considerable sadness amongst colleagues, especially as they'd served closely together for quite some time.

The following day, Ted enquired about Charlie but was informed that he'd been transferred to a hospital at Amiens, then later still it was thought he was returned to England.

......................................

Having been sent from Forceville to Bouzincourt, then back to Forceville again, before ending up at Englebelmer, the 51st – or what was left of them – were ordered to remain in a partially ruined barn on the outskirts of the village until further notice. Each one of them was resentful of the treatment they were receiving, and typically Tommy's no-nonsense approach to the matter might well have been thought of in certain quarters as being a little on the coarse side.

During early evening, on the third day of their barn residency, the lads stood watching the spectacle of enemy artillery as they opened fire in fits and starts on the village. Just as it seemed there was a lull in their activities, one final missile struck the church spire, sending it crashing to earth.

It was the only building in Englebelmer to have remained untouched, but now some subnormal moron, with a compelling urge to destroy for the hell of it, had sent this beautiful architectural creation into senseless obliteration.

Had this horrendous war really become so ungodly that any act of evil was now accepted as being permissible?

# CHAPTER 32

## Spanish Flu

As the spring of 1918 drifted into summer, exploits along the British Front appeared to have reached an unnatural standstill. Rumours were circulating which suggested that Fritz was concentrating his efforts against the French, some progress having been made on the River Aisne both east and west of Reims.

By the 18th July snippets of information were being passed down the line of a great French counter-attack which took the invader completely by surprise, and which meant he'd miscalculated the situation. Unfortunately, however, the French suffered extremely heavy losses, causing many observers to predict that France, as a military force, was at the end of its tether.

What a good job that General Foch thought otherwise, for he struck even harder at the astounded enemy, recovering considerable amounts of lost ground in rapid time.

On the front where the 17th Division was operating, a few sharp raids were carried out by both adversaries and aeroplanes from each side flew high above taking photographs of gun positions and troop movements. Occasionally, aerial battles would take place with the cheers or boos from Tommy, depending on who the successful combatant was.

The lads were well aware it was the calm before the storm and that very shortly the new boys from Blighty, who'd been rushed out to reinforce those divisions who had lost so many old hands, would know what it was like to follow in the footsteps of the glorious dead.

Huge ammunition dumps were being constructed for several miles behind the line, while fresh trenches were dug by Chinese labour squads. In fact, everything being put together suggested something of great significance was about to happen.

Just as front-line divisions were anticipating orders to make a massive all-out assault on the enemy, an unprecedented phenomenon occurred to cause postponement of any predicted action which Haig and his advisers had planned. It had nothing whatsoever to do with adverse weather conditions or even superior German defences – but instead a large-scale epidemic of what became known as Spanish Flu.

Spreading as fast as a 'Fen farmer's muck-knocking elbow', it was so contagious that every division in the British Sector was drastically affected.

Having returned to trench duty just a little earlier, Captain Squires was one of the first victims of the virus, but on the following day almost the entire 51st TMB became so ill that stretcher-bearers were called in to carry them to awaiting ambulances, some five hundred metres behind the line.

Consisting of Lincolns, Sherwoods, Borders and South Staffs, the 17th Division became so decimated by the epidemic, their remaining men would not have been sufficient in number to put up an effective defence had the Germans attacked. Fortunately, however, it was confirmed later that they too were experiencing identical problems.

Sent to a forward Dressing-Station at Acheux-en-Amiénois, where hundreds of men remained for one night only, Ted woke up to find his mate Harold Stokes lying next to him, but both of them were so ill they couldn't find the energy to engage in conversation. Early next morning, a large convoy of ambulances moved them to a military hospital at Gézaincourt, just a short distance from Doullens.

Upon arrival it soon became obvious that medical staff were experiencing great difficulty in coping with such a sudden influx. Wounded men had to be transferred to Boulogne and then returned to Blighty before the influenza victims could be given proper treatment. Even then, every ward was packed to capacity, with the majority of patients being from the 17th Division.

Ted had never felt so desperately ill in his entire life and obviously the same applied to every man affected. But what worried them most of all was that quite a number of invalids were dying from the disease.

Suffering with nausea and exhaustion, Ted was just one of a hundred or so who were instructed to return to their battalions after a mere ten days in hospital. Space was desperately needed for fresh casualties and subsequently a high-ranking medical officer thought it couldn't harm them further by rejoining their units.

Meeting up with the 7th Lincolns who were resting at Hérissart, Ted and his mates were hoping to spend at least another week in clean straw on a barn floor well away from the stench of sickness and diarrhoea, which they'd experienced for twenty-four hours a day in hospital. Such wishful thinking was not to be for Ted, however, for he was awakened next morning by a lance-corporal delivering the post.

Opening the first envelope which he realised was from sister Eadie in Market Harborough, he was flabbergasted to learn that his father had died two weeks earlier.

Writing to ask if it was at all possible for him to get compassionate leave, as not only would his presence be a boost for their mother who was still mourning the death of Frank, but also to try and unscramble their father's business affairs.

To make matters even worse, Eadie had also sent a telegram a day earlier than the letter, and no one had taken the trouble to ensure that this had been delivered. To say that Ted was annoyed by such incompetence was akin to someone waving a red rag to a bad-tempered bull.

Taking advice from Lieutenant Glen, he composed a letter to Battalion HQ requesting leave urgently, and giving the reasons why.

With characteristic unconcern a reply was not received until a week after the funeral had taken place. It was short and without compassion. *'Death of a family member is not sufficient reason for leave to be granted at this particular time'*.

At that very moment in time, Ted found himself loathing everything associated with the British Army, especially those self-opinionated high-ranking officers who managed to spend so much time at home in Blighty themselves.

Being the victim of injustice, Ted discussed the matter of his unacceptable situation with a group of mates and each one agreed that it was little wonder the army's hostile 'couldn't-care-less' policies toward Tommy didn't cause far greater disgruntlement. But it was Harold Stokes' typical no-nonsense approach which summed up the matter quite accurately, when he said, "Well you know what them self-centred sods are like; they just bugger off back to Blighty at the drop of a bloody hat, if somebody back home writes and tells 'em the bloody cat's off colour… but we've got to accept that we're only bloody gun-fodder… we're not supposed to have feelings."

Before the Spanish Flu epidemic decimated the ranks of all divisions, the great German offensive had been brought to an abrupt halt. Fritz had indeed advanced rather spectacularly, recapturing towns, villages and important strongholds, but growing numbers of reinforcements were being brought in to bolster the Allied build-up and Jerry was beginning to feel decidedly jittery.

The great resurgence of endeavour gradually gathered momentum, until on the 8th August 1918, the Australians met with considerable success east of Amiens. The strategy, it seemed, being for them to press forward as quickly as possible before being relieved by one of the battalions from the 17th Division.

Reaching Méricourt on the 13th August, the 7th Lincolns were allocated the task of trench-holding. It was so quiet, everyone assumed that the Germans must have retreated much further than originally thought, so a great many of the lads decided to sleep in the long grass in the grounds of a nearby ruined chateau.

As midnight arrived at the end of the second day, the troop contingent were rudely awakened by the sound of bursting shells, though seemingly nowhere near as powerful or frightening as those used during normal front-line conflict.

To begin with there were no ear-shattering explosions only heavy thuds, and it wasn't until a lone voice shouted "gas" that the realisation of what was happening caused any kind of reaction.

Unable to put their respirators on quickly enough, many were very quickly in considerable trouble, and for some time, men were panic-stricken. For what remained of the night, those who'd been caught unprepared were coughing and spluttering like sheep, struggling to free some impure substance from their throats.

What a sorry sight the chateau grounds were when dawn broke. Desperately fighting to stabilise their breathing, men of all ranks were suffering dreadfully. Even Major Peddie, second in command of the 7th, was caught unawares and he too was in a pretty poor condition.

Of the one hundred and twenty men who were affected by the gas, only a handful returned to line duty. Several of them were mates of Ted and he neither saw nor heard of them again.

Joined by reinforcements, those who survived speedily recovered from their ordeal and in next to no time they were able to play their full part in getting rid of Fritz from French soil once and for all.

# CHAPTER 33

## The Captain's Tipple

Brought up to full strength the 17th slipped into the line close to Aveluy Wood, five kilometres or thereabout north of Albert. During previous encounters this well-known name had been a veritable death trap for the division, but now the enemy was on the run and the only Germans to be seen were dead ones. Orders received from Divisional HQ were concise: "Attack and hold, Attack and hold".

Carrying out their task with customary accuracy, the artillery lads managed to wipe out large groups of one hundred or more retreating combatants with just one salvo. Caught without realising how vulnerable they were, their colleagues had no time to bury them, such was their desperation to disengage.

In the high hot sun, it was always possible to tell when and where such slaughter had occurred as the repulsive stench, together with the sight of huge swarms of hovering flies, was the infallible evidence detectable at two hundred paces.

At sunrise on the 23rd August, the division waded across the River Ancre and together with the 21st Division, they pursued a disheartened enemy. Hundreds of demoralised prisoners were captured without any semblance of blows being exchanged, this being totally alien to the tenacious fighting spirit we had come to expect of the Germans.

Within next to no time, Thiepval Ridge was back in Allied hands. Stuff Redoubt and Courcelette, both notorious battlegrounds during the 1916 campaign, were also taken, but once again the renowned German stubbornness when on the defensive was rarely encountered.

During the first Somme battle, the Lincolns had fought over this very same ground, but in those days it was more to do with trench-holding than being involved in all-out attack. Almost all those original Lincolnshire lads were high-spirited Kitchener volunteers, but sadly a great many of them were no longer around to tell the tale.

Halting for no more than a couple of nights at a time, it was a twin-pronged attack which saw the fall of Le Sars and Martinpuich, before converging to take Flers and Guedecourt, a few kilometres south of Bapaume.

What a desolate wilderness everywhere was. Shell holes every few metres away from each other posed great problems, and more often than not they were half-full of dead Germans, who when utterly exhausted and struggling for breath, dropped into them in a last-ditch attempt to cheat the inevitable.

Sunken roads were shattered into all shapes and sizes resembling the aftermath of seismic activity, while lines of abandoned trenches, zigzagged across the defoliated terrain. Worst of all was the distressing sight of ruined villages, once the pride and joy of so many happy householders.

The infantryman's journey through such manmade stumbling blocks was far from straightforward and every now and again, enemy artillery would open up causing fatalities.

News was received of outstanding advances being made right across the British Sector, in fact so much so that it was at times difficult to know exactly where the line was. It also seemed that Fritz was retreating at speed and our enthusiastic lads were hell-bent on pursuing him.

Still operating below Bapaume, the division occupied Le Transloy and Rocquigny at full throttle, which if nothing else, proved just how ineffective the enemy had become. Tommy was now well aware that he was fighting a winning battle and Jerry knew he was losing one.

..................................

During the overnight respite at Rocquiqny, Captain Squires unexpectedly returned to frontline duty and when he accidentally bumped into Ted, he held out a hand and greeted him like a long-lost friend, not officer and private.

"Well, well, you old devil, I'm so pleased to see there's no truth in the rumour."

"Rumour, sir? What rumour might that be, sir?"

"Well now, a week or so back, I was told a bullet had your name on it."

"That's funny, sir, as I was told you were still in hospital in Blighty, sir."

The two of them laughed and shook hands again before the captain moved off with Lieutenants Clark and Dexter.

Once out of sight, Ted's mates reappeared and began to pull his leg mercilessly. Once again, the captain's renowned unorthodox approach to rank protocol had caused a bit of a stir.

..................................

Later that day playing cards with his mates, Ted was interrupted by an orderly who informed him that Captain Squires wished to see him immediately.

Entering a somewhat woeful makeshift office, the captain called out, "Ah there you are… I've got rather an important job for you."

Saluting like any good soldier of Kitchener's volunteers, Ted replied, "Er, important job sir?"

"Yes, I've just been in conversation with the Battalion CO and he tells me we are in urgent need of certain supplies, so I've jotted down a list of needs and I want you to take it as quickly as you can to Lincolnshire Transport HQ."

"But that's a dozen or so kilometres away sir… I won't get there tonight."

"No, I know you won't but just do your very best. I'm relying on you."

"Yes, sir… very good, sir."

Just as Ted turned to go, the captain said, "Oh, by the way on your return I'd like you to pop into Albert and pick up half a dozen bottles of my favourite tipple. I'm sure you know which brand I prefer." The officer then pushed a wad of francs into Ted's hand and wished him bon voyage.

..................................

Wishing to cover as much ground as possible before nightfall, Ted scurried around shell holes and jumped disused trenches like someone possessed, often attracting humorous comments from the multitude of troopers either going towards the line or leaving it.

With dusk fast approaching he decided to rest up for a few hours in what he believed was a rather large but somewhat worse-for-wear garden behind what seemed like an equally large but ruined chateau.

Propping himself up against what he assumed was a broken statue, he soon fell fast asleep, but upon emerging from his world of sinister nightmares sometime around daybreak, he was staggered to find that he'd spent the night in a large unsightly cemetery.

Lying on top of their hallowed mounds, many of the corpses were of British infantrymen. Some of the older skeletons were broken haphazardly with bones and pieces of bone strewn all over – what a gruesome sight it all was.

Using 'borrowed' bicycles, lifts with passing army vehicles, as well as a great amount of reliance on Shanks's pony, he eventually arrived at his destination.

A corporal was on the point of directing Ted to the OC's office when someone emerged from a wooden storeroom and called him by name. At first he didn't recognise the officer rushing towards him and it wasn't until they were within a few feet of each other that he realised who it was – Lieutenant Alf Wiggins, previously CSM and sergeant and before that Private Alf Wiggins, one of the Saddle-Room gang.

Ted and Alf were good pals in pre-war days, Alf working on the Easton Estate, no more than a good stone's throw down the Great North Road from Buckminster. The pair of them enlisted on the very same day and did their training at Lincoln and Bovington together.

Providing Ted with a welcome meal, Alf wished to know all the news from the lads in 'B' Company. Instructions were then given to a sergeant to arrange for two lorry-loads of requisitions to be transported to Rocquigny, and he was also able to provide the half-dozen bottles of Captain Squire's favourite tipple, as well as an extra one for Ted's own use.

Because of the dreadful ground conditions, Ted took on the role of navigator in the leading vehicle. Arriving at their destination almost a whole day later, they were informed that the 7th Battalion had moved in the direction of Gouzeaucourt, taking both Ytres and Fins on the way, apparently against little or no opposition whatsoever.

Snatching forty winks as the supply lorries pulled up, everyone was highly delighted to see them as the items on board had been in short supply for quite some time, but Alf Wiggins had made certain that his old mates would at least dine fairly well that evening.

Captain Squires congratulated Ted on a job well done and for his troubles gave him one of his own bottles of Scotch.

Thanking the captain, Ted 'forgot' to mention that Alf had also pushed an extra bottle into his haversack before leaving Transport HQ, and in any case, his particular group of mates would appreciate two nightcaps apiece instead of just the one.

# CHAPTER 34

## Poor Old Tom

By the time September 1918 had arrived, it was fairly obvious that the enemy was no longer the well-oiled military machine of the previous four years. Not that their demise was to be taken for granted, as they were at times, still able to retaliate strongly even when back-pedalling at speed.

The 51st TMB were operating under the administrative command of the 17th Division and this meant that only two mortar guns were allocated to each battalion within that division.

..................................

While being kept in reserve, the 7th Lincolnshire bivouacked midway between Rocquigny and Barastra. Sitting down alongside an old trench, Ted and a group of lads were quietly talking amongst themselves when a corporal from early 'B' Company days called to Ted, "Bad job about poor old Tom," to which Ted replied, "Tom who?".

Within the following few minutes Ted learned the full gory details of his good mate's unexpected death; the good mate being no other than Tom Armstrong. Tom was the second member of the three pals from Buckminster to lay down their lives for King and Country – the trio having enlisted on the same day at Grantham Barracks four years earlier.

Working alongside each other on the Dysart Estate, where they lived in the Hall Garden's Bothy, they'd also both played for the village football and cricket teams, as well as visiting the Dysart Arms together, but now only Ted was left. All of a sudden he felt totally devastated.

**Tom astride one of his beloved horses**

......................................

Upon leaving the village school at thirteen, Tom had begun working with horses and when the position arose for him to take up the post of groom to a staff officer in the 15th Battalion, Durham Light Infantry, he was overjoyed.

Engaged in front-line trench warfare for most of his time in Belgium and France, Ted amazingly came through unscathed, whereas Tom who'd acquired what he himself admitted was a cushy number, well away from the actual fighting, now lay dead. A stray long-distance shell had blown him up, together with his beloved horses as they lay asleep in a stable in the village of Lechelle, no more than three kilometres from where Ted was billeted.

......................................

Finishing its reserve period, the 7th was under orders to rendezvous with the other battalions which made up the 17th Division, before moving closer to the line.

The lads were joking about the difficulty of knowing exactly where the line was supposed to be, but an unexpected salvo of artillery fire caught them unawares, leaving very many dead and dying.

A solitary German machine-gun was causing considerable problems for the advancing 7th, but Lieutenant Clark brought the two mortars into the action and in next to no time they disposed of the troublemaker. There was much friendly banter between the two crews, and whereas Ted always claimed it was his gun that was responsible for destroying a certain target, so too did the other crew, led by Frank Waterton.

Coming into view across a long ridge of high ground was a considerable number of German infantrymen, each with hands raised high. Leading them was a high-ranking officer and by the time they reached the lads, it was obvious they were exhausted and extremely hungry.

With the enemy in disarray, the 7th Battalion was meeting with only irregular resistance and British divisions seemed to be falling over each other to bring the sabre-rattling to an end.

By the end of the month the 17th moved in a north-easterly direction, recapturing Trescault and Havrincourt, before turning westward to take possession of Hermies. At this particular stage, however, there was very little evidence of enemy participation, although they had been seriously restricted by a shortfall of men, ammunition and food supplies.

Welcomed with open arms, it was easy to understand such euphoria being displayed, as the villagers had suffered beyond all measure under enemy occupation. In fact, inhabitants told the lads that Fritz had only withdrawn a few days earlier and the general consensus was one of good riddance.

The 17th Division were the very first Allied troops the villagers had set eyes on for four long years. Just imagine what fear and intimidation they must have had to tolerate on a daily basis, and also how they must have felt when, at long last, they saw their liberators approaching. After having almost given up hope of ever being released from the awful chains of despair, they could at last move freely throughout their village, able to stop and talk to other inhabitants without fear of retribution.

.....................................

Managing to put a considerable distance between themselves and British troops, Jerry was still intent on creating as much mayhem as possible, for every so often he would send over a sudden simultaneous outburst of shellfire in the hope of causing distress amongst his pursuers

Fired in desperation, his accuracy left much to be desired, but within a short time of the division leaving Selvigny a lone missile came whistling over killing two Sherwood Foresters and injuring many more.

Passing through Selvigny, Caullery and Montigny, the division then came under orders to rest up between Caudry and Audencourt.

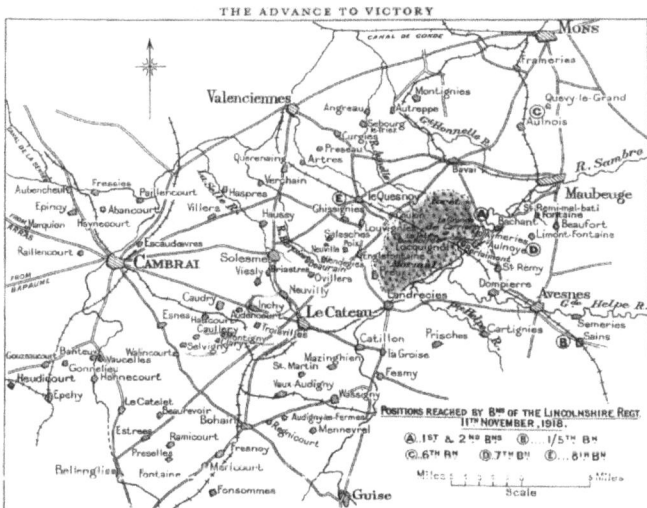

THE ADVANCE TO VICTORY

**Mormal Forest where Ted last saw action**

..........................................

# CHAPTER 35

# Roundabout Route to Inchy

With the arrival of October persistent rumours circulated amongst British troops that the Germans were on the brink of collapse. Knowing that Austria, Bulgaria and Turkey had requested peace terms, Tommy being Tommy, assumed that Hindenburg would very quickly be doing likewise on behalf of his countrymen. But of course, German dogged determination was made of much sterner stuff than that of its allies, and so for the time being anyway, they defiantly carried on regardless.

For want of something better to do, the 7th Lincolnshires carried out a so-called purposeful training programme, although the lads repeatedly wished to know why.

According to front-line officers, it was supposed to be for the benefit of young eighteen-year-old second lieutenants who had only recently arrived from England. Naturally, the infantry lads, having been on active service for anything up to four years, didn't appreciate such ill-considered army policy, and Tommy's colourful choice of expletives with which he vented his feelings about the matter made officers, NCOs and Uncle Tom Cobley an' all, squirm in their highly polished boots. To Tommy, of course, it didn't seem to matter who he offended by such inelegance of speech – if Sir Douglas Haig himself had been within earshot, he would have been treated to the very same repertoire.

Communications between the different divisions who had been brought in to administer the last rites to the German army weren't always what they should have been. Subsequently, it almost became a case of the left hand not knowing what the right hand was doing. In fact, some military objectives were being captured by one battalion, without other field-commanders knowing, thereby causing another battalion to carry out an unnecessary repeat assault the following day.

To be fair, however, this had as much to do with adverse weather conditions as it did with grand strategy. And all British troops involved knew full well that Fritz was on his last legs and they all wanted to be involved at the death.

The weather had been deteriorating for the past week or so, but towards the end of the month, it was causing considerable problems for both the infantry battalions as well as the artillery boys.

On the 28th October, the 7th Lincolnshires were moved from canvas billets just outside of Audencourt to canvas billets just outside of Troisvilles, close to Le Cateau, a town which was only unshackled from enemy occupation a few days earlier by the 31st Division.

When allowed to visit Le Cateau the lads found it to be a stimulating place, although its estaminets were closed due to them having little or nothing to sell.

Virtually untouched by the savage brutality of war, the town centre retained its distinctive French features, whereas its outskirts had suffered immensely. The lovely cathedral remained undamaged in spite of the invaders placing mines throughout its entire structure, in readiness to effect its obliteration when the last of the occupation forces made their planned getaway. Thankfully, however, they found themselves with insufficient time to carry out their macabre threats, thus enabling a mentally sharp priest to alert the British military, thereby saving the entire edifice from total destruction.

Returning to canvas city, the two trench mortar crews were approached by Captain Squires, who told them he had a special job he needed them to carry out.

"Special job, sir?" queried Ted and Frank Waterton.

Sensing a dissatisfied reaction, the captain snapped, "Yes, a special job. Do you have a problem with that?" No one replied.

"Right then, it seems we are required to give mortar assistance to the 37th."

"The 37th sir?" chorused the lads, rather derisively.

"Yes, the 37th and I want you to be ready to move out within the hour. Lieutenant Clark will fill you in with the details."

..................................

Complaining bitterly amongst themselves about the injustices of army life, the eight lads openly cursed their misfortune as only sophisticated young Tommies knew how.

It was raining cats and dogs when the lorry carrying two mortar-guns and an ample supply of shells pulled out of the temporary camp, where the Lincolnshires had bivouacked for the past two days. Lieutenant Clark sat in the front with the driver, while the lads made the best of their lot, sitting in the cramped space behind.

"Any idea where we're going, sir?" called Ted.

"Neuvilly," replied the irritable officer, implying that he too wasn't best pleased about the situation.

Nothing further was mentioned for some time, until Frank Waterton stirred himself and casually muttered, "Neuvilly. I bet that's bloody miles away."

Every few yards shell craters affected the vehicle's progress and when the heavens really did open, it made any form of reasonable navigation virtually impossible. Therefore, it came as no surprise when pulling into what was thought at the time to be the outlying districts of Inchy, the officer decided to stay put overnight.

Coming to a halt halfway along what was assumed to be the village street, it was noticed that most of the properties were damaged in some way or another. Broken roof tiles were strewn everywhere, while doors and windows were conspicuous by their absence.

Entering a dilapidated barn, the eight lads plus the driver dossed down wherever was convenient, although Lieutenant Clark decided to take his chances in the front of the lorry, which had been parked slightly further along what was supposed to be a road.

The barn was by no stretch of the imagination the ideal place in which to spend the night, but the lads agreed, they'd spent nights in worse. Having managed to snatch a couple of hours' inactive drowsiness, the small group were rudely awakened by the threatening sound of exploding shells landing in close proximity.

Rushing out of the building at breakneck speed Ted, Arthur Perrins and Frank Waterton frantically attempted to put some distance between themselves and the makeshift sanctuary just as another missile struck the doorway from which they'd emerged. The blast was so powerful it threw them to the ground with considerable force. Dragging themselves slowly upright, Ted and Arthur were about to continue their panic-stricken, mad-dash getaway when they realised that Frank was unable to move, having been hit by flying shell fragments.

In a nearby empty outhouse, Ted and Arthur managed to cut open one of their mate's trouser legs, where they found deep lacerations from thigh to ankle. Trying their utmost to patch up the gaping wounds with field dressings and tatty net curtaining, which they wrenched from one of the windows, they were, after some considerable time, able to congratulate each other on a job well done.

Having made their wounded colleague as comfortable as possible, the two of them cautiously made their way back to the barn, just as Lieutenant Clark surfaced from his deep slumber in the front seat of the lorry. It appears he had heard little or nothing of the commotion, so it was only natural he wished to know full details, but neither Ted nor Arthur could ill afford the time to enlighten him there and then.

Striking matches to try and get a clearer view of the task ahead of them, the trio worked tirelessly in an attempt to claw their way through the huge pile of rubble, with the officer being put in the picture, as the great struggle against time continued.

Fortunately for the TMBs, a Borders' Battalion was awaiting orders close by, and following a short discussion amongst themselves, about a dozen or so wandered along to try and find out where the sudden disturbance was coming from – and what a tremendous difference their input made.

Once those hard-working lads had made their way through the blockage, the trapped five were quickly traced. Unfortunately, however, two of them were dead, having become victims of falling debris, while the other three, although injured, were able to converse with their rescuers.

Appearing on the horrifying scene of destruction and carnage, stretcher-bearers immediately took control of the situation, carrying out running repairs on the wounded men, while at the same time, encouraging them into believing that everything would very soon be as good as new. Comforting words indeed, especially as they had badly shattered limbs and blood trickling into their eyes from head wounds.

Loading the three injured lads into an awaiting ambulance, together with Frank Waterton, of course, the four stretcher-bearers waved goodbye to the onlookers before disappearing into the darkness of a cold, wet, very early morning. When Ted mentioned what a marvellous job those lads had carried out everyone nodded in agreement and a Borders' Corporal remarked that he wouldn't have done it for all the tea in China.

Upon checking his map, Lieutenant Clark informed Ted and Arthur that the long, eventful journey which the pair hadn't stopped complaining about was actually no more than three kilometres away, as the crow flies. Both lads remained adamant that if that were the case, then they must have gone via Paris!

Ruined buildings on the road to Inchy

After considerable soul-searching the officer decided to carry on to Neuvilly with just Ted and Arthur, in the hope that additional men could be called upon to assist with the guns and missiles once they'd been able to locate the 37th, as ordered by Captain Squires.

The journey to Neuvilly was an eventful one and the two privates never stopped complaining –slipping and sliding all over the place, it took over three hours to complete the three kilometres to their destination, only to be informed upon arrival that Neuvilly had been captured by the 50th Brigade several days earlier.

Learning that the 7th Lincolnshires had now turned up at a place called Poix-du-Nord, in readiness to enter Mormal Forest with the 51st Brigade, Lieutenant Clark decided to head in that direction, as it was only two kilometres further eastward.

Passing through the ruined buildings of Ovillers, large groups of British troops were loitering around, seemingly not knowing whether they were supposed to be coming or going. The truth of the matter was, there were so many different divisions close to the forest that they were more than likely getting in each other's way.

Every front-line soldier, irrespective of rank, was very well aware that victory was just around the corner, and the outcome of the fast-approaching battle could make it sooner rather than later.

The River Herpies, between Beaurain and Vandegies was in flood, and on top of this there was a horrible blend of heavy rain and thick mist. Far from ideal conditions for covering a landscape which was alien to the TMB trio.

Against all odds, the lorry eventually entered Poix-du-Nord, but by the time contact was made with the 51st Division, they were informed that the 7th were by now in the region of Englefontaine, which was still another kilometre eastward alongside Mormal Forest.

.....................................

When informed who the motley looking trio were, a somewhat short-tempered captain shouted, "Where the bloody hell have you emerged from? You look as if you've spent a night in a pigsty half full of shit. Don't you know there's a bloody war on?" As Lieutenant Clark tried to explain the problems they'd encountered on the way to Inchy School, he was abruptly cut off in mid-sentence with a critical admonishment ringing in his ears.

"I have no time to listen to your pettifogging excuses lieutenant. You know as well as I do that dress standards must be maintained at all time."

Yet again the lieutenant attempted to intervene, only for the pompous, over-officious troublemaker to yell, "Just get out of my sight all three of you, and don't let me catch you looking like street urchins again, or you'll be for the high jump."

Seething inwardly, the lieutenant and the two privates saluted and did an about turn, before marching off into the thick mist. Disgusted with the captain's inconsiderate outburst, the lieutenant said, "The bloody stupid bastard, who in God's name does the pig-ignorant know-it-all think he is."

Before going off to try and find a senior officer of the 7th Battalion, the lieutenant suggested to his two mortar gunners that they should try and grab something to eat at one of the field kitchens before the three of them met up again back at the lorry within the hour.

Fed, watered and washed, the trio did meet up as arranged, only for Lieutenant Clark to inform Ted and Arthur they'd been given an immediate assignment.

It seemed the troops allocated the task of clearing the enemy from Mormal Forest were anticipating problems from two separate sets of farm buildings alongside perimeter fencing, as it was known they were both occupied by Germans. Even more worrying was the fact that they were known to have the use of machine guns.

Together with the assistance of a guide as well as three dozen infantrymen, they made their first halt no more than a kilometre away, alongside the forest boundary, as their first target came into view through breaks in the mist.

It seemed the buildings were used by Fritz to create delaying tactics, in order to enable their troops to have more time to escape.

As each shell struck its objective, the enemy's resistance quickly came to an end.

Hoisting pieces of dirty white cloth to indicate surrender, as many as twenty Germans with hands held high, trudged disconsolately away from the battered building, each one looking fear-stricken.

Entering the two-storey structure, the infantry lads quickly came across another dozen or so, so badly injured they were unable to walk. Stretcher-bearers moved in rapidly and in next to no time, all of the injured were taken by ambulance to a dressing station on the road to Le Cateau.

Another such stumbling block on the forest side of Raucourt-au-Bois was given identical treatment, and again its occupants also capitulated without putting up any resistance.

...................................

At 5.30am on the 4th November, the 7th Lincolnshires entered the forest, south of Gay Farm, with the Border

Regiment on their right and Sherwood Foresters on their left. It was almost pitch dark, and extremely cold and foggy into the bargain. In fact, the fog had become so thick, troops were fast becoming dispersed.

By now, enemy artillery was well aware that an assault was in progress, and in a last desperate attempt to prolong the inevitable, they sent over a very heavy barrage. And, of course, in this they included a fair sprinkling of smoke shells, causing even more confusion amongst advancing troops.

Many good men were killed that morning, and because of the dreadful conditions, all the British lads could do was to tuck themselves in tightly behind tree trunks and keep their fingers crossed.

Barely moving when following the so-called advance, at which they thought was a reasonably safe distance, Lieutenant Clark, Ted and Arthur Perrins took immediate evasive action, abandoning their lorry at the very moment the first shell came screaming over.

Lying in a cold, wet, muddy ditch, alongside the rough stone and clay forest ride, the trio waited almost twenty minutes before the barrage ended, and what a daunting sight greeted them.

Their lorry had been the victim of a direct hit and subsequently both it and its contents were now completely inoperable.

Upon closer inspection of the distorted mess, Lieutenant Clark didn't quite know whether to laugh or cry, for what had proved to be highly effective weaponry was now neither use nor ornament.

It wasn't as if Fritz's gunnery boys had pinpointed the lorry as a worthwhile target; a stray shell had somehow struck lucky. Continuing to stare at the smouldering metal, it wasn't until the officer said, "I reckon it might be a good idea if we abandon ship, before our obnoxious captain friend puts in an appearance and orders us to get the whole lot cleaned up."

Having committed the worst sin in the British Army, that of losing their rifles, both Ted and Arthur were in full agreement. Moving no more than two dozen metres amongst a cluster of oaks, the three of them stumbled over several fallen comrades, thus enabling them to 'borrow' a rifle apiece, as well as a quantity of ammunition.

There were a great number of Tommies in the forest, all trying to move forward at a snail's pace, sometimes not even that. Not one of them daring to open fire, as no one was able to tell if any movement ahead of them was made by friend or foe.

Eventually, the mist lifted, enabling the Lincolnshires to regroup, before making a determined all-out effort to reach the eastern boundary of the forest. At this point, however, the Germans were putting up stiff opposition, especially as our own artillery was unable to help out due to ground conditions, following the prolonged heavy rain.

Later, Fritz's aggression had noticeably subsided, so much so that on the evening of the 8th November, the Lincolnshires were informed that the enemy had abandoned their line.

Orders were received to advance again and within a short period of time, during the early hours of the 9th November, the 7th moved clear of the forest. Their immediate target was a place called Beaufort which they entered, along with numerous other battalions, without any form of opposition whatsoever.

By this time no one had any idea what to do next, as rumours amongst the lads were widespread that the armistice would be signed that very day.

Relieved by the 52nd Brigade, the Lincolnshires returned to billets in Aulnoye, close to Mormal Forest.

# CHAPTER 36

## The Long March

Although the depleted TMB crew weren't actually aware of it, the destruction of their vehicle and mortar-guns in Mormal Forest was the very last time they took part in any meaningful activity during the war.

Still hindered by intermittent showers and a thick swirling ground mist, as well as a smattering of 'heavies', the 7th Lincolnshires had at last been able to move out of the dense woodland on the 9th November.

Receiving orders to advance on the same night, they moved into Beaufort, midway between Avesnes and Maubeuge.

Greeted by a British patrol who informed them that the Germans had already retreated at speed, it was a case of 'where do we go from here?'

Awaiting further instructions, they were relieved by troops of the 52nd Brigade and with no clear orders looming, the battalion returned to billets in Aulnoye. It was here that they heard of the signing of the armistice.

At precisely 11am on the 11th day, of the 11th month 1918, the Lincolnshires received news that the war had officially come to an end. Several other battalions were in close proximity and each and every member, irrespective of rank, was out and about celebrating on the streets of Aulnoye.

Privates were shaking hands with lieutenants, while corporals did likewise with sergeant majors. The Lincolnshire lads were back-slapping Sherwood Foresters, while The Borders were attempting to teach

Scottish reels to the French inhabitants, who'd joined in the revelry.

Unfortunately, not one estaminet was open for the sale of drinks, so the rest of the day turned out to be something of a damp squib. Nothing to celebrate such a mind-blowing moment in time, as the men of all ranks would have wished – what a disappointing anti-climax it all was.

Cold, wet and hungry, the only people who seemed to show concern over their plight were members of the native population; the British generals and their high-ranking flunkeys being far too busy over indulging themselves to worry about such trifling matters as Tommy's well-being. So it was still only bully and rock-hard biscuits on the menu, but as Tommy said, "Don't worry about it, mate – we'll all be back in Blighty by this time next week."

.............................

Within a short period of the armistice being signed, communiqués from GHQ were received by all divisional commanders, but not one of them gave cause for celebration.

Tommy had given up to four years of blood, tears and severe hardship fighting for King and Country and those who'd managed to survive were both physically and mentally exhausted. All the lads wanted was to be allowed to return home as quickly as possible, for they had carried out a magnificent task in a 'hell-upon-earth' situation. Kitchener had promised them that as soon as hostilities ceased, they would be returned to their loved ones post-haste, but unfortunately it seems he conveniently forgot to mention it to those who mattered most at GHQ.

..........................

Enlisting within a few days of war being declared, Kitchener's 'New Army' was acclaimed by the British press as being the saviour of mankind, but such high-minded observations only served to antagonise those influential generals at GHQ for no one, absolutely no one, was allowed to steal their thunder. Throughout the entire conflict they were quite happy to let everyone back in Blighty know that if anyone was worthy of high acclaim and appreciation, it was them and not their insignificant subordinates, who only had shells, bombs, bullets, gas and mud to contend with.

.............................

Making absolutely certain that the British Army still had a duty to perform in peacetime France, the politicians in London readily agreed with the generals that it was appropriate for them to remain there for longer than intended.

Front-line officers and other ranks were well aware that senior GHQ generals and their sidekicks didn't know the difference between a dug-out and a brick outhouse, for the simple reason they'd never been within fifty kilometres of the line from day one of the war, right up to the Armistice Day. Now shells and bullets no longer posed a threat, however, they were out and about in towns and villages, where some of the heaviest fighting had occurred.

Taking the salute at many stage-managed parades, not once were they seen without an official photographer in attendance, in order to record the occasion for posterity. What a great opportunity for them to show off their rows of medals, despite not one of them being won on the field of battle.

During the whole time the war was taking place, it was Tommy more than anyone who took the risks. It was Tommy who went over the top. It was Tommy who was gassed. It was Tommy who suffered horrendous wounds, and more often than not it was Tommy who paid the ultimate price.

Regrettably, front-line Tommy rarely received any form of recognition for the superb job he'd carried out in the most appalling conditions imaginable. Yet those pompous buffoons at GHQ, who had never even fired a rifle in anger, always managed to emerge with the honours.

...................................

Following four weeks of playing at being peace-time soldiers, Tommy's spirit sank even lower and it was virtually impossible to persuade him to take the least possible interest in anything other than matters relating to the all-absorbing topic of demobilisation. Mere grumbling to NCOs about the acrimonious situation gradually turned into open hostility towards their officers, but of course, it wasn't their fault that the unscrupulous manipulators had put their own aspirations above those of Tommy, just because he'd received certain assurances at the time when Britain's armies so desperately needed recruits.

Being made aware of the men's feelings, the CO must have worked wonders behind the scenes, for within a short time, he had all his battalions called out on parade and told them they were to be moved closer to the Channel ports in readiness to be shipped back to England. But even then, GHQ had the last laugh by making it crystal clear that no transport would be made available to take them. So on the 7th December, the 17th

Division began the long 150-kilometre march to the town of Abbeville, roughly midway between Arras and Dieppe.

Considered to be the best way of seeing the French countryside in peacetime, none of the lads appreciated the seemingly never-ending foot slogging, especially after what they had given to their country's cause over the previous four years.

Passing through a great many villages, some unrecognisable as such, due to the saturation shelling they'd endured, the never-ending khaki columns were enthusiastically greeted with hand-clapping, hand-shaking and back-slapping, almost all throughout their long, emotional journey – it was the inhabitants' way of saying: 'goodbye Tommy and thanks for everything'.

Surely those charming French people deserved a far better life to the one they'd been obliged to lead over the past four years; A life in which they could move around freely from dawn to dusk, without fear of being stopped by enemy security forces. And they most definitely deserved a future in which their young children could sleep contentedly every night.

Wholeheartedly singing all the old favourites, the lads inevitably returned to *Take Me Back to Dear Old Blighty*, for this was indeed the one song in their extensive repertoire, which meant so much to them.

Reaching the world's largest graveyard known to all Tommies as The Somme, singing automatically came to an abrupt stop, for whichever way the lads looked, multitudes of temporary wooden crosses on the graves of their comrades in arms were still very much in evidence. Unashamedly, tears welled in the eyes of almost everyone, as they remembered old pals who now lay in their interim plots, while awaiting removal to the new official military cemeteries, which were already beginning to emerge in Belgium and France.

Flowing through the windmills of their minds were so many place names, in which not that long ago they'd stood shoulder to shoulder with their mates in cold muddy trenches, wondering if they'd survive to see another dawn.

..............................

Moving back through Mormal Forest, Tommy's marathon march took him through Englefontaine, Inchy, Audencourt, Caudry, Mesnières, Ribécourt, Havrincourt, Hermies, Bertincourt, Barastra, Rocquigny, Le Transloy, Ginchy, Longueval, Fricourt, Méaulte, Morlancourt and Sailly Laurette, then along the course of the Somme River to Corbie and Neuville, before stopping at Amiens for three days. Across countryside which would have made an excellent assault course, it had taken a week to get there with overnight stops in derelict houses en route.

Eventually, the Abbeville area was reached and Ted found himself with the 7th Lincolnshires in billets at Érondelle. Here, the lads spent Christmas and the New Year, patronising well-stocked estaminets. Sometimes, however, they visited Pont-Remy and Eaucourt-sur-Somme, but almost always they finished up in some form of drinking establishment.

With precious little to occupy their minds, not unlike all other battalions in the British Army, they became totally bored with their present way of life. The longer than anticipated return to Blighty for their final release was well over schedule, so yet again, questions regarding such an incendiary matter erupted whenever and wherever groups of Kitchener's lads gathered.

..............................

When not feeling in the best of moods, Tommy's language was, more often than not, rather colourful to say the least and he didn't seem to give a damn who heard him either. On this particular occasion, they were all of the same mind, with their range of indelicate phraseology going full blast – and for once, their own battalion officers and senior NCOs shared similar sentiments.

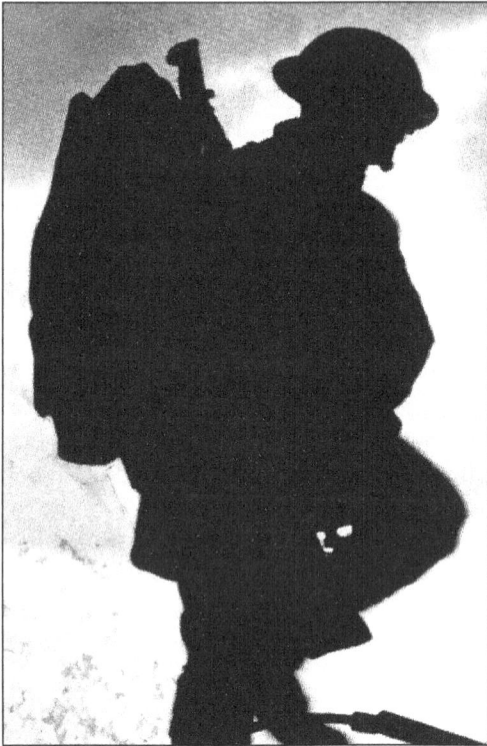

# CHAPTER 37

# Journey's End

The 18th of January 1919 became one of the most memorable days of Ted's life, for it was the date he received official notification from Brigade headquarters concerning his demobilisation.

During the previous forty-eight hours, every man in the 7th Lincolnshires had been warned that the ruling regarding release from military service was entirely dependent upon the length of time spent in front-line duty. Having served longer than most, Ted eagerly anticipated being amongst the first batch to be returned to civilian life, and he was highly delighted when on the following day, he was just one of a hundred or so to be instructed to march to Epagne in order to receive a compulsory medical examination. Soon afterwards, they all had to undergo a ninety-kilometre journey in a convoy of lorries to Brigade HQ at Rouen.

Arriving at their destination just before nightfall, they were given a reasonably decent meal before being directed to overnight billets on the outskirts of the city.

Returning to HQ next morning, the lads were heading towards the demobilisation centre where they were handed their official release papers, although they were made aware that their final documents would not be issued until the military authorities back in Lincolnshire were satisfied that all army equipment was returned in a satisfactory condition.

Le Havre was the next port of call, but upon arrival, they found the place jam-packed with men of every regiment imaginable, all of them awaiting embarkation to Blighty.

It took two whole days before the Poachers were able to board their boat, which was appropriately named *The Nirvana*. Deriving from primarily Buddhist and Hindu religions, it means 'the ultimate state of spiritual tranquillity, attained through release from every day concerns'. For those now on board who'd borne so much suffering and wretchedness on a daily basis for so long, it couldn't have been more apt.

Dropping anchor a mile out of port, the heaving mass slept as best they could in readiness to set sail for Southampton at first light.

.................................

It was the sudden vibration of the boat's engines which stirred the sleeping cargo; every one of them awkwardly scrambling to their feet, watching the French coastline gradually disappear into the mists of time, making the moment almost seem as if the horrors of the past four years were merely figments of their imagination.

Packed in like sardines in a can, *The Nirvana* made its way slowly up the Solent causing a spontaneous full-volume cheer as the docks suddenly came into view. As the mist lifted especially for the occasion, it was really wonderful to be able to see dear old England again.

.................................

Upon reaching the town's railway station, members of the Salvation Army had laid out an impressive feast of sandwiches and cakes et cetera, solely for Tommy's benefit. It almost seemed too good to be true, but how the lads appreciated it.

Insufficient recognition was given to the Salvationists contribution to the war effort, but just ask any Tommy how he rated their worth and he'd say, "they were the best of the bunch – simply the best."

.....................................

It was the 26th January 1919, when the special train steamed out of Southampton to commence its northbound journey, passing through Basingstoke, Oxford and Leicester, prior to arriving at Nottingham's Victoria Station at 10.55pm.

Staying overnight at the YMCA, the party of Lincolns returned next morning where they boarded another 'special' heading for Grantham. Then it was a march through the town, to the demobilisation centre at Harrowby Camp.

Completing two full days of typical army official procedure, which every returning Tommy regarded as pure baloney, the lads were finally handed their release documents, as well as their very last payment, before being allowed to leave as civilians again.

Back-slapping and handshakes galore took place before the various groups separated to catch their different modes of transport to all corners of the county, as well as a few such as Ted who were heading for places beyond its border. Each and every one was fully aware this was the final parting of the ways – a typical scenario which would be performed by all returning groups of Tommies, of every regiment between Land's End and John O' Groats.

Although Ted was the first of the four surviving brothers who'd served in the BEF to arrive back home, it somehow seemed strangely unsettling. Pleased as she so obviously was to have her son returned safe and sound, his mother still appeared to be suffering from some form of emotional distress, quite understandable considering she'd lost a son and husband within a period of sixteen months.

Demobilised within the following three weeks, brothers Arthur, Harry and Fred seemed to give their mother a renewed sense of purpose in life, which made it considerably easier for Ted to be able to raise the matter of his impending departure to Buckminster, in order to resume his chosen career.

...............................

The village was recovering well from the aftermath of a severe winter as Ted rhythmically pedalled his bicycle along the main street, having ridden it from Melton Mowbray railway station. Stopping every so often to acknowledge old acquaintances, it merely substantiated what he already knew in his own mind – that this was the place where he hoped his long-term future might be.

Riding alongside the twelve-foot-high brick garden wall, the sun pushed its way through an overcast sky to make a welcome appearance.

Alighting to lift his cycle through the small green wooden door, which was an integral part of a much larger one, Ted paused for a moment or two to give thought to that September morning four and a half years ago, when along with Humphrey and Tom, he'd ridden off to Grantham Barracks to enlist in Kitchener's army. Pedalling their cycles along the Crabtree Road, then on to the Great North Road, the happy-go-lucky trio were expecting it all to be one big exciting adventure. It was certainly never intended to turn out the way it did, and Ted was now left on his own to reflect just why his two best mates should be lying in some foreign field, while he himself went through hell on earth so many times, yet came through it all completely unscathed.

From the direction of the head-gardener's office, an elated voice called, "Hello there, Ted. Good to have you back."

"Good to be back," he replied.

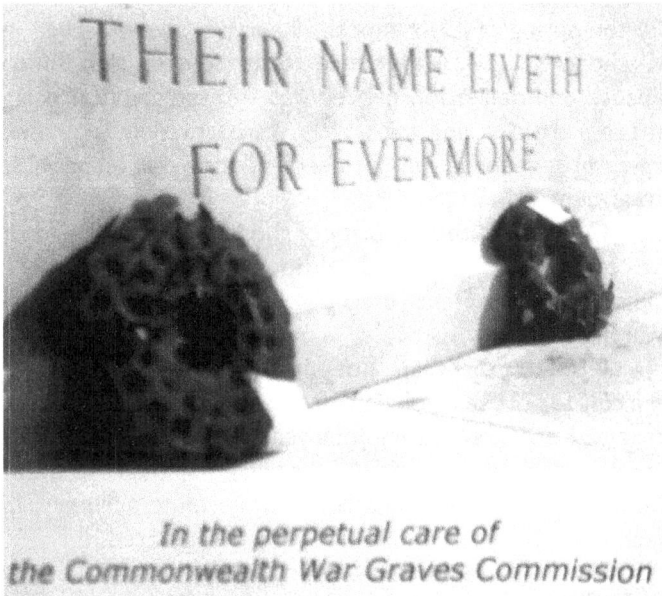

THEIR NAME LIVETH FOR EVERMORE

In the perpetual care of the Commonwealth War Graves Commission

# EPILOGUE

By the spring of 1919 almost all survivors who served in Kitchener's New Army were repatriated to the UK to finalise demobilisation procedures – the exception being those heroic young men who were severely wounded and subsequently still in need of long-term specialist treatment.

Outwardly, the majority of those released looked to be completely revitalised, although in reality, a more sinister predicament emerged: the legacy of trench warfare.

More often than not, it was consciously quite difficult for those involved to remember every little detail that had occurred during four years or so in the line, but in the nocturnal world of horrific nightmares, every incident was often re-enacted with absolute accuracy. In fact, if anything they were hideously exaggerated.

The nightmares, however, not only haunted Tommy but NCOs and front-line officers alike, and if the truth be known, so too did the very same frightening hallucinations appear on the nightly stage of almost every returning German infantryman.

Tossing and turning in his unadorned sleeping quarters at the bothy, Ted too was troubled by the lifelike intrusions.

Disturbed enormously by the evil spectre of Humphrey and Tom's mutilated corpses as they rode headless white horses across no man's land, he would awake to find himself calling out their names. Also appearing nightly was the haunting tragedy of brother

Arthur desperately trying to stem the flow of blood coming from Frank's appalling wounds, made considerably worse by stretcher-bearers being unable to reach them due to their legs being firmly stuck in a sea of mud. To make matters seem even worse, it would sometimes involve a role reversal whereby Arthur was on the receiving end of an exploding shell, and it was Frank who would be desperately trying to attend to his wounds.

Sometimes, the nightmares would involve Ted being the last man standing at Thiepval Ridge, facing hundreds of advancing enemy soldiers with bayonets fixed.

Barely a night would pass without him stumbling over the dead and dying in Delville Wood, or find himself hanging upside down in a trench full of dirty brown water.

So very many times he relived the dreadful deaths of Lieutenants Hayward and Shankster – two extremely fine officers whose nightly presence caused considerable heart- ache. And nearly always, close mates such as Jasper Houghton, Frank Gent, Charlie Wright, John Cooper, Arthur Brayshaw, Percy Welbourne et al, whose gruesome deaths caused such great distress but which became increasingly bizarre as time passed by.

Every one of those fearful nightmares was experienced by every returning front-line soldier, irrespective of rank or nationality. Some of them returned to a near-normal sleeping pattern within months, others took years, while others still, never recovered.

.....................................

Always remember, it is the politicians who decide to make war – but always it is poor old Tommy who fights their battles for them. And whereas not one politician loses their life, a vast amount of front-line soldiers pay the ultimate price.

# Tommy and The Brass

Having finished reading this compressed version of a front-line Tommy's war diaries, you will not have failed to notice that neither he nor his comrades had scant regard for their own generals or, for that matter, any other kind of brass hat.

Doubtless, numerous explanations have been propounded during the past in an attempt to justify why such a sorry state of affairs was allowed to continue throughout a war, in which there were in excess of two and a half million British casualties.

The following observations may help you to understand just why Tommy was so critical of his country's high-ranking officers at a time in our history when trust, cooperation, leadership and loyalty should have been the basic principles with which every serving soldier, irrespective of rank, should have complied.

At the commencement of hostilities, regular soldiers were hastily recalled from foreign parts to help repress the well-planned German invasion of Belgium and France.

Inadequately trained in modern trench warfare, these regulars, nevertheless, performed admirably, while at the same time being well aware that there was a vast difference between fighting adversaries such as the Boers, to becoming involved in a full-scale war against a highly organised military machine.

During his entire army career, the regular soldier was made to accept orders without question, but this all changed when Kitchener's service battalions entered the fray.

Following their baptism of fire, these enlisted men realised that their survival in the line depended a great deal on top brass deploying men and strategy shrewdly. Generalship needed to be of the highest calibre, but unfortunately, Tommy could see very little evidence of this and he wasn't slow in letting all and sundry know about it.

As far as the front-line infantryman was concerned, it was the young officers and CSMs who had served no longer than the enlisted men under their command, who ran things efficiently and it was, more often than not, only when the brass stuck their oar in that serious cock-ups occurred.

This caused the beginning of Tommy's dislike of the brass, yet a great many front-line infantrymen had never even set eyes on one.

As time passed by, Tommy was ordered to carry out increasing numbers of 'over the top' incursions into enemy-held territory. They were invariably the unnecessary, ill-advised brainchildr of those ostentatious, self-admiring backscratchers from GHQ, and mostly they resulted in vast numbers of Britain's finest sons being killed or seriously wounded. Little wonder that Kitchener's volunteers had so little time for them.

Other bones of contention were food, drink, sleeping quarters, leave passes and medals.

For example, often for weeks on end, Tommy was expected to survive on rock-hard biscuits and bully, while the brass were served six-course meals on a daily basis.

When in the line, Tommy's water ration was often delivered in old contaminated petrol cans, which meant that tea when brewed sometimes tasted rather unpleasant. In the meantime, however, the brass were enjoying ample supplies of spirits and the best French wines.

While front-line Tommy spent most of his sleeping hours in trench sides and bottoms or on damp straw on barn floors, senior officers were supplied with double beds in their very own luxurious quarters.

Leave passes were allocated to Tommy as if they were made of gold, yet the brass nipped across the channel to Blighty or often to Paris, at the drop of a hat.

Another shameful inequality which Tommy deplored was the unfair distribution of medals. Infantrymen were continuously coerced into carrying out unbelievable acts of bravery, mostly without any official recognition whatsoever, yet DSOs and MCs were dished out to the brass like large spoonfuls of blancmange at children's birthday parties.

Having stated these facts, it is only right that it should also be acknowledged that there were many high-ranking officers who were both extremely competent as well as empathetic. Such qualities, however commendable, should not have been sufficient grounds to warrant the award of medals for outstanding heroism on a battlefield, especially as the recipients had never been within a good day's march of one.

Certain military historians have, in the past, been unable to accept that there were some high-ranking officers who served in the B.E.F, and did so without being worthy of any respect. What a pity these annalists weren't able to refer to copies of General Crozier's book *A Brass Hat in No Man's Land* or Lloyd George's *War Memoirs*. Had they done so, it may well have changed their opinions.

Brilliantly written, both volumes were highly controversial at the time of publication, but they most certainly gave the British public a more balanced awareness of the disruptions and injustices which had occurred in the higher echelons of military command throughout the conflict.

In General Crozier's book, there was an intriguing narrative about two brass hats being so drunk while on duty that they were unable to carry out their responsibilities. In fact, it seems they were so 'plastered' they became a menace to the safety of the men under their command. After taking a considerable amount of time to sleep-off the after-effects, they were made to appear before a fellow officer's tribunal, who, it was assumed, would mete out whatever penalty was considered appropriate.

Just imagine the ribald laughter in the mess when the two offender's punishment became known. Both were sent back to Blighty to take up a cushy desk job, without any loss of rank, and as a solace to their souls, they were awarded DSOs – so you see, the old school tie really did work wonders. However, as Tommy observed, if the same charge had been brought against a couple of the lads, they would have been convicted on some trumped-up evidence and shot at dawn.

As a consideration: this is exactly what happened to 266 young Tommies during the war. The majority of them had been so drunk they didn't even know what day of the week it was. They were men who'd been under constant bombardment from enemy artillery, often for several days on end. Surely they'd earned the right to have a drink or two if they wanted, but the brass didn't see it that way and denounced such behaviour. Despite the obvious hypocrisy that they themselves were often in a far worse state than Tommy, if they thought he was guilty, it was a bullet through the heart for him.

Tommy abhorred such military rules and regulations and was quick to say so. Mind you, if Tommy was shot at dawn today, even for a far more serious offence, the perpetrators would be charged with murder – and rightly so.

Of course, it's much too late to change the course of history, but do you think Tommy was justified in making such allegations against the brass? Make up your own mind – the jury has already been out for one hundred years on this one.

# Wear a poppy ...
# for the lions killed
# in war, not the
# donkeys who
# send them there

# After the War

Ted returns to his beloved
Buckminster Hall Gardens
as Head Gardener

BUCKMINSTER HALL 7£8

This photo was taken just after the Great War and shows the central structure of Buckminster Hall, which was at that time the Country Seat of Lord Dysart.

During the Second World War it was used as a military convalescent home. It was seriously damaged by a fire in late 1949 and demolished.

Later a new imposing residence was erected on the same site.

# St John the Baptist, Buckminster

This is the Parish Church of St John the Baptist in the picturesque village of Buckminster in which Ted married Margaret Rayson in 1924.

Ted's final resting place on the extreme right of the photo – a far cry from the savagery of The Somme

In Memory of
Private

# Percy Welbourne

19062, 7th Bn., Lincolnshire Regiment who died on 25 December 1917 Age 23

Son of the late Mr. G. and Mrs. F. Welbourne, of 8, New Row, Gonerby Hill Foot, Grantham.

Remembered with Honour
Arras Memorial

Commemorated in perpetuity by
the Commonwealth War Graves Commission

**Percy Welbourne commemorated in perpetuity
Arras Memorial – (See Chapter 27)**

**Tyne Cot Memorial**
**Final resting place of James Suckling**

Unbeknown to his Trench Mortar Battery colleagues, James Suckling did return to active service but was unfortunately killed on 16th April 1918 (see page 183)

In Memory of

Gunner

# Frank Rigby Dunkley

60586, 60th Siege Bty., Royal Garrison Artillery who died on 01 April 1917 Age 25

Son of Henry and Eliza Dunkley, of Market Harborough.

Remembered with Honour
Barlin Communal Cemetery Extension

Commemorated in perpetuity by
the Commonwealth War Graves Commission

**Brother Frank's final resting place –
Barlin Communal Cemetery Extension**
*'Asleep in a Garden of Rest'*

# The Armistice

As the dying embers of the month of October 1918 gradually faded away, all front-line infantrymen, irrespective of rank, couldn't help but notice there was a sudden upsurge in military operations. In fact, on whichever section of the Western Front they were employed, men were beginning to ask the question, "what the devil is going on?" more so especially, as the Allies were experiencing great difficulty in keeping up with a rapidly retreating enemy.

By the time November arrived, the weather had deteriorated beyond all measure, with both heavy rain and dense fog becoming widespread. Ludendorff's finest troops were, by now, thoroughly exhausted, but if the truth was known, so too was Tommy, who had no desire to face another bitterly cold freezing winter of trench-warfare.

As the final few days of that first week of the month expired, rumours galore were circulating as to exactly what was taking place at a supposedly secret rendezvous in the close proximity.

By the 11th November the world learned that war between the Allies and Germany had ended.

It also transpired that a meeting had taken place between belligerent states on the 9th November in Marshal Foch's special train in the Forest of Compiègne, although the actual Armistice document was not signed until 5.10am on the 11th. Even then, it did not come into effect until the 11th hour of the 11th day of the 11th month. And so the war which was supposed to end all wars came to a rather unexpected conclusion.

The carriage in which the Armistice was actually signed remained in the very same location before being removed for renovation purposes. When completed, it was taken to the Cour Des Invalides in Paris, where it was put on exhibition.

In 1937 it was ceremonially returned to the Compiègne Forest site to become the centrepiece of a new museum which had been specially built.

# Footnote

The Armistice carriage remained on this location until the 22nd June 1940, when swastika-bedecked German staff cars bearing Adolf Hitler, Hermann Göring, Wilhelm Keitel and Joachim von Ribbentrop raced into the forest site and demanded the Armistice document. Once this was in their possession Hitler ordered the carriage's removal to Berlin where it was exhibited in the Lustgarten. Following the Allied advance into Germany in early 1945, the carriage was removed by the Germans to the town of Ohrdruf, but as an American armoured column entered the town, a detachment of the SS set it ablaze and it was destroyed.

After the war the Compiègne site was restored, but it was not until Armistice Day 1950 that a replacement carriage found to be correct in every detail as the original was installed.

# Escape From Hell

After the guns had fallen silent
And the trenches had begun to fall in
Tommy yearned to return to Blighty
To seek solace amongst kith and kin.

All that he wished for was to go home
And walk down an English green lane
He'd fought in a war to end all wars
Now he wanted to be a civilian again.

Sailing orders finally arrived
What a glorious day it all seemed
Steaming jam-packed o'er the water,
It was better than he'd ever dreamed.

Blighty again, a dream come true,
Mother Nature preparing for spring;
Newly born lambs frolicking in fields
Skylark singing high on the wing.

What a change from exploding shells
And bullets that whiz past your head
What a change to see animals grazing
Instead of fields littered with dead.

Demobilization, hand-shaking mates,
Puffing-billy passes hamlets and farms
Then it's home to meet up with family
And a Mother's welcoming arms.

*GFD*

Lightning Source UK Ltd.
Milton Keynes UK
UKOW06f0441101214